1980s Project Studies/Council on Foreign Relations

STUDIES AVAILABLE

INTERNATIONAL DISASTER RELIEF:
Toward a Responsive System
Stephen Green

NUCLEAR PROLIFERATION:
Motivations, Capabilities, and Strategies for Control
*Studies by Ted Greenwood and by Theodore B. Taylor and
Harold A. Feiveson*

ALTERNATIVES TO MONETARY DISORDER
*Studies by Fred Hirsch and Michael Doyle and by
Edward L. Morse*

CHINA'S FUTURE:
Foreign Policy and Economic Development in the Post-Mao Era
Studies by Allen S. Whiting and by Robert Dernberger

STUDIES FORTHCOMING

Some 25 additional volumes of the 1980s Project work will be appearing in the course of the next year or two. Most will contain independent but related studies concerning issues of potentially great importance in the next decade and beyond, such as the control of strategic weaponry, resource management, terrorism, relations between the developing and developed societies, and the world market in conventional arms, among many others. Additionally, a number of volumes will be devoted to particular regions of the world, concentrating especially on political and economic development trends outside the industrialized West.

International Disaster Relief

International Disaster Relief

TOWARD A RESPONSIVE SYSTEM

STEPHEN GREEN

1980s Project/Council on Foreign Relations

McGRAW-HILL BOOK COMPANY
New York   St. Louis   San Francisco
Auckland   Bogotá   Düsseldorf   Johannesburg   London   Madrid
Mexico   Montreal   New Delhi   Panama   Paris   São Paulo
Singapore   Sydney   Tokyo   Toronto

The Council on Foreign Relations, Inc., is a nonprofit and nonpartisan organization devoted to promoting improved understanding of international affairs through the free exchange of ideas. Its membership of about 1,700 persons throughout the United States is made up of individuals with special interest and experience in international affairs. The Council has no affiliation with and receives no funding from the United States government.

The Council publishes the quarterly journal *Foreign Affairs*, and, from time to time, books and monographs that in the judgment of the Council's Committee on Studies are responsible treatments of significant international topics worthy of presentation to the public. The 1980s Project is a research effort of the Council; as such, 1980s Project Studies have been similarly reviewed through procedures of the Committee on Studies. As in the case of all Council publications, statements of fact and expressions of opinion contained in 1980s Project Studies are the sole responsibility of their authors.

The editor of this book was Michael Schwarz for the Council on Foreign Relations. Thomas Quinn and Michael Hennelly were the editors for McGraw-Hill Book Company, the designer was Christopher Simon, and Milton Heiberg supervised the production. It was set in Times Roman by Creative Book Services, Inc.

Printed and bound by R. R. Donnelley & Sons

Library of Congress Cataloging in Publication Data

Green, Stephen.
International disaster relief.

(1980s project/Council on Foreign Relations)
Bibliography: p.
Includes index.
1.   Disaster relief.   I.   Title.   II.   Series: Council
on Foreign Relations.   1980s project/Council on Foreign
Relations.
HV553.G69   361.5   76–44414
ISBN 0–07–024287–9
ISBN 0–07–024288–7 pbk.
1 2 3 4 5 6 7 8 9 RRDRRD 7 0 9 8 7

Contents

List of Tables

Foreword

Stephen Green's study of international mechanisms to provide relief for victims of natural disasters is one of many studies to be produced in the course of the 1980s Project of the Council on Foreign Relations. Each 1980s Project study analyzes an issue or set of issues that is likely to be of major international concern during the coming decade or two. Most of the studies go beyond analysis. They seek to describe some of the conditions that would make for a better world, and to propose feasible paths along which progress toward those conditions might be made.

The ambitious purpose of the 1980s Project is to examine important political and economic problems not only individually but in relationship to one another. Some studies or books produced by the Project will primarily emphasize the interrelationship of issues. In the case of other, more specifically focused studies, a considerable effort has been made to write, review, and criticize them in the context of more general Project work. Each Project study is thus capable of standing on its own; at the same time it has been shaped by a broader perspective.

The 1980s Project had its origins in the widely held recognition that many of the assumptions, policies, and institutions that have characterized international relations during the past 30 years are inadequate to the demands of today and foreseeable demands of the period between now and 1990 or so. Over the course of the next decade, substantial adaptation of institutions and behavior will be needed to respond to the changed circumstances of the 1980s and beyond. The Project seeks to identify those future conditions and the kinds of adaptation they might require. It is not the Project's purpose to arrive at a single or exclusive set of goals. Nor does it focus upon the foreign policy or national interests of the United States alone. Instead, it seeks to identify goals that are compatible with the perceived interests of most states, despite differences in ideology and in level of economic development.

The published products of the Project are aimed at a broad readership, including policymakers and potential policymakers but confined to no single nation or region. The authors of Project studies were therefore asked to remain mindful of interests broader than those of any one society and to take fully into account the likely realities of domestic politics in the principal societies involved. All those who have worked in the Project, however, have tried not to be captives of the status quo; they have sought to question the inevitability of existing patterns of thought and behavior that restrain desirable change and to look for ways in which those patterns might in time be altered or their consequences mitigated.

The 1980s Project is at once a series of separate attacks upon a number of urgent and potentially urgent international problems and also a collective effort, involving a substantial number of persons in the United States and abroad, to bring those separate approaches to bear upon one another and to suggest the kinds of choices that might be made among them. The Project involves more than 300 participants. A small central staff and a steering Coordinating Group have worked to define the questions and to assess the compatibility of policy prescriptions. Nearly 100 authors, from more than a dozen countries, have been at work on separate studies. Twelve working groups of specialists and generalists have been convened to subject the Project's studies to critical scrutiny and to help in the process of identifying interrelationships among them.

The 1980s Project is the largest single research and studies effort the Council on Foreign Relations has undertaken in its 55-year history, comparable in conception only to a major study of the postwar world, the War and Peace Studies, undertaken by the Council during the Second World War. At that time, the impetus to the effort was the discontinuity caused by worldwide conflict and the visible and inescapable need to rethink, replace, and supplement many of the features of the international system that had prevailed before the war. The discontinuities in today's world are less obvious and, even when occasionally quite visible—as in the abandonment of gold convertibility and fixed monetary parities—only briefly command the spotlight of public attention. That new institutions and patterns of behavior are needed in many areas is widely acknowledged, but the sense of need is less urgent—existing institutions have not for the most part dramatically failed and collapsed. The tendency, therefore, is to make do with outmoded arrangements and to improvise rather than to undertake a basic analysis of the problems that lie before us and of the demands that those problems will place upon all nations.

The 1980s Project is based upon the belief that serious effort and integrated forethought can contribute—indeed, are indispensable—to progress in the next decade toward a more humane, peaceful, productive, and just world. And it rests upon the hope that participants in its deliberations and readers of Project publications—whether or not they agree with an author's given point of view—may be helped to think more informedly about the opportunities and the dangers that lie ahead and the consequences of various possible courses of future action.

The 1980s Project has been made possible by generous grants from the Ford Foundation, the Lilly Endowment, the Andrew W. Mellon Foundation, the Rockefeller Foundation, and the German Marshall Fund of the United States. Neither the Council on Foreign Relations nor any of those foundations is responsible for statements of fact and expressions of opinion contained in publications of the 1980s Project; they are the sole responsibility of the individual authors under whose names they appear. But the Council on Foreign Relations and the staff of the 1980s Project take great pleasure in placing those publications before a wide readership both in the United States and abroad.

Richard H. Ullman
Director, the 1980s Project

During 1975 and 1976, ten Working Groups met to explore major international issues and to subject initial drafts of 1980s Project studies to critical review. Those who chaired Project Working Groups were:

Cyrus R. Vance, Working Group on Nuclear Weapons and Other Weapons of Mass Destruction

Leslie H. Gelb, Working Group on Armed Conflict

Roger Fisher, Working Group on Transnational Violence and Subversion

Rev. Theodore M. Hesburgh, Working Group on Human Rights

Joseph S. Nye, Jr., Working Group on the Political Economy of North-South Relations

Harold Van B. Cleveland, Working Group on Macroeconomic Policies and International Monetary Relations

Lawrence C. McQuade, Working Group on Principles of International Trade

William Diebold, Jr., Working Group on Multinational Enterprises

Eugene B. Skolnikoff, Working Group on the Environment, the Global Commons, and Economic Growth

Miriam Camps, Working Group on Industrial Policy

The members of the 1980s Project staff are:

Miriam Camps	*Catherine B. Gwin*
William Diebold, Jr.	*Roger D. Hansen*
David C. Gompert	*Edward L. Morse*

Richard H. Ullman (Director)

The Committee on Studies of the Board of Directors of the Council on Foreign Relations was the governing body of the 1980s Project. The Committee's members as of December 31, 1976 were:

The Coordinating Group of the 1980s Project had a central advisory role in the work of the Project. Its members as of December 31, 1976 were:

International Disaster Relief

Introduction

Richard H. Ullman

Natural disasters are, of course, as old as mankind. Floods, famine, fires, disease, and all the other calamities triggered by nature's forces fill the chronicles of recorded history—indeed, along with wars, they were for centuries the principal events by which people marked transitions from one epoch to another. Despite successive technological revolutions, their effects are still with us. their impact sometimes shifted but their toll still high. In "good" years they claim hundreds of thousands of lives, in "bad" years millions.

The years ahead, as Stephen Green warns us, are likely to be bad ones. Judged by what is likely to be the experience of the 1980s, the natural disasters of the 1960s and 1970s may well appear moderate in their effects. Explosive population growth in precisely those societies that are poorest and least able to prepare for or recover from disasters and the continued concentrating of humanity mean that natural events of the same physical magnitude as those of the past will probably wreak much greater havoc. Their consequences will be made even more calamitous by the fact that governments in disaster-struck countries are sometimes unwilling—for reasons relating to both domestic and international politics—to admit to their own people and to the outside world the true dimensions of the horror that is taking place. Thus, by acts of both commission and omission, people add to nature's toll. Stephen Green uses the term *megadisasters* to encapsulate these likely catastrophes of the 1980s. It is neither exaggerated nor overly sensational.

Just as some of the by-products of modernization have led to explosive population growth and drastic stress on fragile ecosystems and therefore have vastly magnified the toll of natural disasters, other forces—also the by-products of modernization—have made possible disaster *relief* as we know it today. The development of long-distance electronic communications permits word of even the most remote natural disasters to reach international relief agencies without great delay. And it is now possible to airlift massive quantities of foods, medicines, and clothing halfway around the globe. The same technology that made possible the large-scale movements of American military forces into remote highland regions of Indochina or of Cuban troops into Angola can bring food, water, and fully equipped emergency hospitals to the victims of earthquakes, floods, famines, and epidemics in Guatemala, Bangladesh, or Ethiopia.

These technologies mean that, in principle, measures to alleviate the distress of natural disasters should be available to all victims of natural disasters: only rarely is it physically impossible, under present conditions, to bring aid directly to the points where it is needed. The obstacles to effective relief—in the 1980s as today—are primarily organizational and political. As Stephen Green makes clear, available resources are often deployed far less efficiently than they might be. Until recently, the international disaster relief "system" has seen no really effective mechanisms for disaster preparedness and for the direction and coordination of outside relief efforts by a multitude of action agencies and donors of resources, some governmental, others private, all with their own particular interests to preserve. In his study, Green describes the beginnings of efforts to create such mechanisms and puts forward recommendations of his own design to make these efforts still more effective.

Green's recommended measures are aimed at alleviating organizational deficiencies that make the effects of natural disasters far more tragic than they need be. But as Green makes clear, there are also political deficiencies. Governments may be too proud to admit to the world that they are unable effectively to feed their populations; they might reckon that desperately needed tourist receipts—not to mention receipts from agricultural exports—would vanish if the seriousness of an epidemic were known; or they may indeed wish to weaken (or punish) a regionally based internal opposition by preventing relief supplies and assistance from entering its region—thus using nature to dispose of opposition that their armies have failed to suppress.

As a means to counter such willful malfeasance, Green proposes an international convention through which signatory states would give recognition to the principle of shared responsibility of individuals and governments for the provision of protection and relief to victims of natural disasters, wherever these victims might be. Such an international agreement would be akin to the 1949 Geneva Conventions on the Rules of War assuring legal protection and material assistance to certain classes of persons involved in armed conflicts. The analogy of the Geneva Conventions is a crucially important aspect of Green's approach to disaster relief. Just as the conventions aim at protecting innocent persons against harm from war, so his proposed convention would aim at protecting them from avoidable harm as a result of natural disasters. Governments of disaster-struck states would not be allowed to prevent relief from reaching the most severely harmed members of their societies, and the provision of relief would be safeguarded against the political whims of donor governments. Relief operations would be routinized, coordinated, and guaranteed.

Disaster relief would thus be considered as a human right; as in the case of any other human right, the accident of birth should not prevent one from its enjoyment. Regarding disaster relief as a human right is consonant with other normative writing in the 1980s Project that argues that all persons have a right to the satisfaction of basic needs for their survival and that all peoples share a responsibility for seeing to it that those basic needs are satisfied.[1] Such a point of view, should it gain currency in the 1980s, would represent a dramatic transformation in international relations—a shift from a primary focus upon relations among states to one instead emphasizing relations among societies. Such a transformation would pose very difficult questions regarding, *inter alia,* appropriate criteria for "legitimate" intervention into what are customarily regarded as the domestic affairs of sovereign states. Such a shift in perspectives would reflect increasingly widespread dissatisfaction with the constraints posed by the recognition of sovereign national

[1] "Basic human needs" have been a central focus of other work in the 1980s Project, and several Project studies now in preparation deal with various aspects of assessing and providing for them. Thus, one study attempts to define "absolute poverty," assesses its magnitude worldwide, and proposes means of eliminating it. Another study focuses on the problem of providing at least minimally adequate levels of nutrition for the world's population. And a third study addresses the problem of establishing culturally neutral indices to measure the degree to which different societies meet the basic needs, and safeguard the rights, of their populations.

jurisdictions. At a time when many governments claim to regard certain geophysical spaces—the ocean bottom, for example—as "the common heritage of mankind" and thus as domains above and beyond national appropriation, it is fitting that human life also should be viewed as mankind's common responsibility and not as a commodity to be needlessly forfeited to the abstract notion of national sovereignty.

Green is, of course, under no illusion that the articulation of this principle and its codification in an international convention would be sufficient to assure the end of the malfeasance he describes. In his paper he proposes steps through which adherence to such a convention might over time be promoted, but he is aware that the process of gaining acceptance and effective enforcement of the principle of common responsibility—and therefore of a right or duty of international intervention on behalf of disaster victims—will be protracted.

Like so many issues of the 1980s, disaster relief will emphasize the inequitable distribution of wealth among nations. For disasters affect most those who are unprepared for them, and even moderate wealth buys some measure of preparedness. Thus, the largest numbers of victims of natural disasters will be citizens of the poorest countries, and disaster relief—involving, in most instances, transfers of resources from rich to poor nations—will not escape from entanglement in the complex politics of what has come to be called "North-South relations." Stephen Green proposes that disaster relief be taken out of the context of "charity," where it has largely been, and that instead a coordinated international relief system should be viewed as a concomitant of development, emphasizing preparedness and prevention but assuring relief where preparedness proves inadequate. The more that relief comes to be regarded as a right rather than as charity, the more the issue may be insulated from the vicissitudes of the overall North-South relationship. Achieving such insulation, however, requires confronting head on some of the thorniest aspects of relations between developed and less-developed states.

One such aspect concerns "delinking." The argument is frequently made, by analysts and publicists both within and outside the developing societies, that in order to achieve patterns of development more in the long-range interests of Southern societies, the developing countries should sever many of the bonds that link them to the North. Particularly pernicious, the argument goes, are those links that perpetuate political and psychological dependencies. Although most spokesmen for the developing world recognize that steady economic growth is dependent upon increased commercial and financial interactions with the North, the kind of interaction favored is of an arms-length nature; forms of foreign assistance that underscore the patron-client character of North-South relations and that leave the Southern states at the mercy of the political whims of less-than-steadfast patrons are resented, if not rejected.

The recognition of the need for capital, technology, and skills from developed economies together with the rejection of dependency as a political condition has led, *inter alia,* to demands that foreign assistance be made both more multilateral and more automatic—i.e., less tied to the national decision-making procedures of donor countries. On the donor side, for obvious reasons, the demand for greater automaticity in foreign assistance has not been enthusiastically embraced. Automaticity would reduce, if not eliminate, the political leverage that presently goes along with bilateral grants of aid. Such leverage has been used as a means both to win friends and to undermine enemies and as a way to exert managerial control over the disposition of assistance funds. It is not likely to be readily given up, not only in cases of long-term technical assistance but even as related to short-term food aid and other forms of disaster relief.

The developing states, for their part, tend to view their vulnerability to disasters as an integral part of the syndrome of "the development of underdevelopment." Consequently, they are unlikely to accept the notion that they "owe" something in exchange for disaster relief. Actually, at first glance no quid pro quo would appear necessary; because of the ubiquitous, random, and visibly lamentable nature of natural disasters, disaster relief appears more susceptible than any other form of international assistance to depoliticization. Yet (rich) donors are likely to require precisely what (poor) recipients are least likely to want to give—access to their societies. In recent years, governments of developing countries have thrown up formidable barriers against efforts by Western journalists and social scientists to report on events within their societies, alleging that outsiders—especially Western outsiders—emphasize negative aspects rather than "objectively" report the achievements of the regime in power. Moreover, there is every indication that restrictions on the flow of information both out of and into Third World societies will grow more severe rather than abate.

Seen as a human right, disaster relief cannot be allowed to be impeded by the political sensitivities of elites in power who might be willing to trade avoidable losses of life for continued incumbency; for the covering up of official incompetence or of unsavory domestic conditions that could retard tourism, trade, and foreign financial transactions; or for the more sinister purpose of undermining domestic opposition. Indeed, disaster relief raises the problem of access in a particularly salient way: relief agencies and governments of donor states are likely to want guarantees that they will regularly receive the kind of information that would assure credible assessments of potential impending disasters (e.g., mass starvation), of the extent of human suffering and thus of the dimensions of assistance needed in the event of an actual disaster, and of the use that the stricken society has made of relief resources that have been provided. Such assessments—to be credible—could come only from the kind of probing, backed up by reports from journalists and other independent observers, to which Third World governments are likely to be most resistant. But it is difficult to imagine that a reformed disaster relief system of the sort Green envisions can function in the absence of an open and free flow of information among societies. Indeed, that is why provisions for guaranteed access would be a central feature of the international convention he proposes.

A final observation: Another initial product of the 1980s Project, along with Green's work on disaster relief, will be a volume focusing on the problem of the proliferation of nuclear weapons.[2] The juxtaposition is fitting. Natural disasters—their effects greatly magnified by human omissions and commissions—and nuclear explosions together constitute much of the range of catastrophic threats under which mankind lives. They are reminders of the fact that despite great progress in many spheres, the work of generations can be disrupted or even destroyed in a brief moment by natural forces or by forces of humanity's own creation. Both underscore the ultimate fragility of the human condition, and the inadequacy of the nation-state as means of guaranteeing personal safety and survival. The vulnerability of some states in the face of natural disasters is an indication that they are unable to provide for other aspects of the security of their citizens, just as no state is able to protect its citizens against a powerful nuclear force. In each instance, arenas for decision making larger than that of the nation-state may come to seem appropriate—in the nuclear case as a means of curtailing the use or the

[2]Ted Greenwood, and Harold A. Feiveson and Theodore Taylor, *Nuclear Proliferation: Motivations, Capabilities, and Strategies for Control,* McGraw-Hill Book Company for the Council on Foreign Relations, New York, forthcoming.

possession of weapons, in the case of natural disasters as a means of making concrete the principle of shared responsibility.

These similarities should not be pressed too far, however. As other work in the 1980s Project makes clear, the process of moving forward toward a world without nuclear weapons will be formidably difficult.[3] But, as Stephen Green's paper shows, a considerably better system of disaster relief could be achieved without major changes in the pattern of world politics. In particular, the principle of common responsibility for aiding victims is one for which acceptance is likely to be forthcoming. The 1980s will be a period marked by the beginnings of international (or transnational) society in a number of spheres but of resistance in a number of others. No single formula will be controlling, either in disaster relief or in any other realm.

[3]A forthcoming volume in the 1980s Project will contain a set of studies dealing with the problems involved in limiting the use and the deployment of nuclear weapons and in eventually eliminating them altogether.

International Disaster Relief

Stephen Green

ONE

The Problem

The Ethiopian famine had almost run its course by late August 1973, when I visited a feeding center called Mersa in one of the country's most decimated areas. People in this northern region had been dying of hunger for months before any food or medical attention became available. But for the last 30 days a Canadian missionary nurse, assisted by local district officials, had tried to stem the dying.

More than 2,000 people sought help at Mersa. The night before I arrived, 22 had died. Although the nurse had medical training, she could not minister to the sick, for she had no medications. Since there was not enough food, she had to ration it to already starving people. Moreover, with no one to relieve the nurse at night, the intravenous fluid bottles that fed the near-dead could not be changed; she "lost" many of the dying during her few hours of sleep.

In the interests of efficiency, the nurse had grouped the Mersa center's population according to their relative health and spent most of her time with those severely malnourished victims who could still be saved through her treatment. She had adopted, then, a form of *triage* known to battlefield doctors for centuries. Even though such measures seemed necessary under the circumstances, as a missionary she was deeply disturbed by them. As a human being, she was angry with the Red Cross, the United Nations, the Ethiopian government—in short, with everyone who she thought should have been doing something to prevent or mitigate the suffering and death.

We walked around the center together, and when we stopped, the nurse wiped her forehead and looked out over the sea of rags and bodies. "You know," she said, "We have laws against stealing and parking in the wrong place. Why don't we have laws against this?" She was not, of course, speaking of the natural elements that had precipitated the crisis. Rather, she was referring to the need to avert the politically caused delay and inefficiency that had contributed to the Ethiopian toll. And Ethiopia's ordeal was not an isolated instance. There is a growing appreciation among the people, organizations, and governments that make up the international disaster relief system that many major disasters—including those we call "natural"—are to a considerable degree manmade. Poor planning, politically motivated neglect, and bad administration often vastly augment the suffering caused by droughts, high winds, floods, fire, and fissures in the earth.

Traditionally hampered by inefficiency and errors of judgment, disaster relief has also been imperiled by more insidious forms of political intervention. Governments in disaster situations often have made decisions not according to the interests of disaster victims but rather in light of perceived political imperatives. They have denied the existence of a disaster. They have steered relief to one ethnic group rather than another. They have given aid on the basis of perceived diplomatic benefits rather than according to the needs of the victims. They have profited enormously from the sale of relief goods.

Disaster victims must be protected from the consequences of such decisions, in order that relief operations can be carried out as quickly and efficiently as possible. Whether this can best be done by "laws"—treaties and the like—or by informal arrangements among governments and organizations is one of the major subjects of this book.

During the 1980s, with the populations of disaster-prone areas continuing to rise, with prospects of food and energy shortages and adverse climatic change, there is reason to believe that human failings will exact a greater toll as increasingly large areas of the developing world become vulnerable to disasters of a scale hitherto unknown. In turn, these "megadisasters" will create conditions of political instability and, in all likelihood, of conflict, which will further erode the capacity of societies to cope with natural disasters. It is this prospect that makes the organization of an effective disaster relief system so imperative today. Indeed, there may well be a need for "laws" against the avoidable human elements of disasters, for in the 1980s, today's disasters may seem small in retrospect.

Beyond the political difficulties associated with international disaster relief there are fundamental management problems. In the late 1960s and early 1970s, major disasters occurred frequently, and the number and size of agencies involved in relief operations grew. This growth, however, was accompanied by waste and duplicated efforts. As the mass media's coverage of disasters increased in scope and depth, so did the accusations of inefficiency. The result has been a trend toward international relief "coordination." Several new committees and one new agency were established to harmonize the emergency relief efforts of the various multilateral government and private organizations. Yet even these changes have failed to improve the system significantly. True, the smaller relief operations tend to be more efficient than the major ones, and the sudden disasters are usually handled more smoothly than the long-term ones. But even today, food, medicine, and clothing often do not reach the people who need them, or they arrive too late to save lives and suffering. The reasons why these changes have been so ineffective will constitute another major focus of this book.

The recent famine in Ethiopia was one of several concurrent natural disasters, regional in nature, involving tens of millions of people and many hundreds of thousands of deaths. Yet the significance of these disasters is not in their size; the world has seen larger catastrophes. Nor is it unusual that several happened simultaneously; this, too, has occurred in the past. Rather, the unsettling aspect of these emergencies—in Bangladesh, the Sahel, and East Africa—is the fact of certain underlying similarities. Each disaster arose from causes that appeared to be irreversible, at least over a short period of time. Each has resulted in political revolution. And each still lingers, in the sense that many experts now speak of "permanent emergencies" in these three areas.

The very concept of permanent emergencies underlines the shallowness of the traditional forms of disaster relief. For decades, people in industrialized nations have responded generously to human tragedies in the less developed nations. Almost always, however, their aid has been spasmodic: a simple, sudden transfer of money, food, supplies, and equipment. Whether the disasters were wars, earthquakes, or longer-developing famines and epidemics, relief operations tried to alleviate victims' dramatic, immediate needs.

Still primarily geared to one activity—the transfer of funds, supplies, and equipment from one place to another—the international disaster relief system does not always serve well the interests of disaster-stricken countries and their people. In fact, it has itself become a kind of permanent emergency. Some steps have already been taken to deal with both the natural elements of disasters and exacerbation of these crises caused by inadequate human responses. The following pages will examine what still needs to be done.

TWO

Patterns in Recent Natural Disasters

The study of global patterns and effects of disasters must be an exercise in inference, for accurate data on these matters simply do not exist. Those who have been in the field have some idea of the necessarily crude, haphazard ways in which existing "statistics" on disasters originate. Nevertheless, certain trends can be discerned—trends that help explain why the consciousness of the world community about disasters and disaster relief has been raised considerably in recent years.

INCIDENCE AND SIZE

The number of natural phenomena that can cause disasters did not increase significantly in the late 1960s and early 1970s. The Center for Short-Lived Phenomena (CSLP), formerly a part of the Smithsonian Institution, has detailed the frequency of some of these phenomena in a recent report (see Table 1).

Though disaster-related natural phenomena do not appear to be increasing in frequency, there is evidence that the human cost of disaster worldwide is steadily mounting. One recent study of global trends in natural disasters has observed that disasters covering large areas and disaster-related deaths have been rising continually from 1947 to 1973.[1]

[1]Judith Dworkin, "Global Trends in Natural Disasters 1947–1973," Working Paper No. 26, Natural Hazard Research Program of the Institute of Behavioral Science, University of Colorado, Boulder, Colo., n.d.

TABLE 1
Types and Numbers of Events
Reported by the Center for Short-Lived Phenomena,
1968–1974

	1968	1969	1970	1971	1972	1973	1974	Total
Geophysical Events								
Volcanic eruptions	12	18	22	19	16	20	19	126
Earthquakes	18	29	19	20	16	14	16	132
Landslides, landslips, and avalanches	1	7	2	2	4	1	3	20
Storm surges, floods, and tidal waves	1	4	4	2	6	8	2	27
Total	32	58	47	43	42	43	40	305

SOURCE: The table is extracted from Table I, p. 15, *1974 Annual Report, Center for Short-Lived Phenomena*, Cambridge, Mass., 1976. Since completing this report, the CSLP has left the Smithsonian Institution and is now a nonprofit corporation providing scientific reports on natural phenomena on a subscription basis.

Total global figures for recent years for damage, deaths, numbers of persons affected, and assistance provided are truly startling. A U.S. Mission to the UN press release indicated that from 1964 to 1973, there were 430 natural disasters worldwide (an average of 1 every 8.5 days), resulting in 3.5 million deaths, some 400 million victims, and $11 billion in damage.[2]

These figures, which are based upon statistics developed by the Office of Foreign Disaster Assistance of the U.S. Agency for International Development (AID/FDA), may be conservative, however. AID/FDA global estimates for total new disasters, people killed and affected, and amounts of international and self-help assistance for fiscal years 1965–1975 are included in Appendix A. They show 112,000 people killed worldwide by disasters in 1973, which is less than one-half the number that same year for Ethiopia alone, according to revised Ethiopian governmental estimates. Similarly, the AID/FDA figures report $32 million in global international assistance for 1974, though the Ethiopian government reported over $100 million in assistance for the Ethiopian famine alone. And—in contrast to the 1964–1973 *worldwide* damage

[2]Joseph M. Segel, press release, U.S. Mission to the UN, USUN 153 (74), October 30, 1974.

16

figure of $11 billion—the Development Assistance Committee of the Organization for Economic Cooperation and Development (OECD) has estimated the typhoon damage in Southeast Asia alone from 1960 to 1970 to have been $9.96 billion.[3]

AID/FDA staff members recognize well the limitations of their data. Their statistics are derived partly from reports of governments in disaster-stricken countries and partly from on-site inspections of remote areas. Thus, the figures are not always systematically computed and frequently cannot be verified. Moreover, even in those cases where accurate estimates are in fact possible, political reasons may lead governments to minimize, exaggerate, or otherwise distort their statistics.

While the frequency of disasters themselves has remained fairly stable, disaster relief has become a "growth enterprise." The League of Red Cross Societies coordinated international assistance in over 300 natural disasters from 1919 through 1974, but most of this activity was in the last 25 years.[4] The USAID Foreign Disaster Relief Coordinator's Office has provided aid simultaneously to as many as 27 foreign disasters. Similarly, the United Nations Disaster Relief Coordinator's Office (UNDRO) is regularly engaged in as many as five or six disaster relief operations at the same time.[5]

Population increases, combined with the pronounced tendency for people worldwide to concentrate in cities and towns, have increased the trauma of disasters. Especially in Africa and in South Asia, many relatively new population clusters have accumulated more or less "naturally," without planning or the sanitation, transportation, health services, and other infrastructures that usually accompany the growth of towns and cities in wealthier, industrialized countries. The results are populous communities vulnerable to disasters.

Still other reasons underlie the severe consequences of natural disasters. One of these, noted by Lester Brown, is the occurrence of "ecological overstress," most notably in huge areas of sub-Saharan Africa and the Indian subcontinent.[6] This term describes the combined effects of population growth, overgrazing, deforestation, and air and water erosion of the land, which all contribute to and exacerbate Africa's almost

[3]David Holdsworth, *Present Role of the Red Cross in Assistance*, Background Paper 3, Joint Committee for the Reappraisal of the Red Cross, Geneva, 1975, p. 77.

[4]Ibid., p. 31.

[5]UN General Assembly Document A/9637, June 5, 1974.

[6]Lester Brown, *By Bread Alone*, Praeger, New York 1974, pp. 10–11.

continuous drought/desertification and India's floods. In the next decade we may see the development of a relatively new phenomenon—the regional disaster, involving numerous countries simultaneously. In both Africa and South Asia, the size of the areas and the numbers of people in the vulnerable zones are staggering; they present logistic and other problems that already exceed the capabilities of the international disaster relief system.

Global climatic changes may also help cause regionwide disasters. U.S. Central Intelligence Agency studies suggest that the major crop failures of the mid- and late-sixties and early seventies in the Indian subcontinent, West Africa, and even the Soviet Union were part of an apparent global trend of adverse climatic change involving generally cooler temperatures and very uneven rainfall patterns, bringing alternate periods of flooding and drought.[7]

At the same time that the scope and effects of disasters are growing, modern technical capacities have made relief operations more feasible. Advances in communications and transportation have contributed to the size and frequency of relief efforts by alerting the world earlier and more graphically to the needs of a disaster-stricken people. Satellite photographs and telephone hookups can convey an accurate assessment of damage in a very few hours. Jet air transport can move relief equipment and supplies in a few more hours. Full-scale international relief operations can be and have been mounted in a matter of two or three days, as they were in the spring 1976 Guatemalan and Italian earthquakes.

TYPE AND LOCATION

The UN Disaster Relief Coordinator mobilized some assistance for 66 separate disasters from March 1972 to March 1976 (see Table 2).[8]

The UNDRO list is, of course, only a very rough indicator of incidence by disaster type. It is also doubtless incomplete, since there are many disasters—particularly human-caused (conflict) disasters—in which UNDRO does not become involved.

While a natural typology for disasters does not exist, a more useful

---

[7]*A Study of Climatological Research as It Pertains to Intelligence Problems,* Office of Research and Development of the U.S. Central Intelligence Agency, August 1974.

[8]UN General Assembly Document A/10079, May 6, 1975, and A/31/88, May 12, 1976.

TABLE 2

Incidence of UNDRO-Assisted Relief Operations According to Disaster Type, March 1972–March 1976

	Number of Occurrences
Floods	27
Cyclones and hurricanes	11
Epidemics	7
Droughts	7
Earthquakes	5
Hostilities and civil disturbances	4
Fires	3
Volcanic eruptions	1
Landslides	1
Total	66

one than the simple list of phenomena given in Table 2 can be created by grouping disasters according to the problems they pose for relief efforts: *sudden disasters,* such as floods, cyclones and hurricanes, fires, earthquakes, volcanic eruptions, and landslides; *slow-developing natural disasters,* such as droughts and epidemics; and entirely *human-caused disasters,* such as international wars, civil wars, and genocide.

The sudden disasters account for 48 of UNDRO's 66 occurrences. These disasters require a quick response (three to four days, usually by air) if the relief is to be of any real use. Since such disasters have effects that are clearly the result of natural phenomena (except in the case of fires), the affected government is usually quite willing to acknowledge that they have occurred. Whatever "political" problems may develop usually arise after relief operations have commenced. These include overblown assessments of supplies and equipment needed, inequitable distribution of relief goods among regions or religious or ethnic groups, and corruption in the administration of relief. Since these disasters usually lack political trauma and are of relatively short duration, relief operations tend to be comparatively successful and the adverse effects on the development process generally minimal.

Slow-developing natural disasters account for 14 on UNDRO's list. (This small number does not reflect the relative importance of this category, for many of these disasters involve large areas and huge numbers of people and cause severe damage.) Very often, people and their governments are accomplices to the natural phenomena in this type of disaster. Overgrazing and tree cutting may exacerbate the effects of drought. Poor sanitation practices and the absence of any health services infrastructure may trigger or worsen an epidemic. For these reasons, political sensitivity and even instability commonly accompany such disasters and often result in delays, inefficiency, and further damage. In turn, the suffering and dying worsen the political crisis, creating a cyclical effect. Perhaps the best example of such a disaster is the Ethiopian drought/famine/revolution/civil war that began in 1973, in which a slow-developing disaster set back a country's development for years.

One reason for UNDRO's not becoming involved in human-caused disasters, such as those attributable to civil wars or genocide, is that political problems that prohibit, delay, or distort the relief operations almost always occur during such situations. In these cases the UN often chooses, in the words of its Charter, not to "interfere in the affairs of a member state." These disasters are the most multidimensional of all, with aspects and implications that are psychological, historical, social, and legal, among others, as well as political and economic.

The geographical distribution of the disasters in UNDRO's list is shown in Table 3. Perhaps the most disturbing pattern of disaster occurrence is the frequency with which they hit the very areas and countries that can least afford to have them. If we combine the original UN list of 25 least developed countries with the (1975) United Nations Emergency Operation (UNEO) list of 33 countries "most seriously affected" by the world economic situation, we arrive at a list of 44 nations. Of the 44, a total of 23, or 52 percent, appear on UNDRO's list of countries that had major disasters requiring international assistance during the four-year period 1972–1976. Actually, several disaster-stricken countries do not, for one reason or another, appear on UNDRO's list. So, in fact, 28 countries from the combined list—or 64 percent of the poorest countries in the world—suffered major disasters requiring international assistance between 1972 and 1976. As Dr. Arnold Rorholt, a former Chief of the Disaster Preparedness Bureau of the League of Red Cross Societies, has said, "In general . . . disaster-

TABLE 3
Geographical Distribution of UNDRO
Relief Operations, March 1972–March 1976

	Number of Disasters
Africa	24
South and East Asia	15
Latin America	12
Middle East	8
Pacific territories and islands	4
Europe	3
Total	66

prone areas are identical with developing areas: poor countries with considerable political, social and particularly economic problems.''[9]

This combined list of countries is included in Table 4. Countries suffering disasters are in italics, and asterisks have been placed by the names of those countries that had disasters but did not appear on the UNDRO list.

TABLE 4
Disaster-Stricken Countries among the World's Poorest Nations

Afghanistan	Democratic Yemen	Khmer Republic*	Rwanda
Bangladesh	El Salvador	Laos*	Senegal
Bhutan	Ethiopia	Lesotho	Sierra Leone
Botswana	Ghana	Madagascar	Sikkim
Burma	Guinea	Malawi	Somalia
Burundi	Guyana	Maldives	Sri Lanka
Cameroon, United Republic of*	Haiti	Mali	Sudan
Central African Republic	Honduras	Mauritania	Tanzania, United Republic of*
	India*	Nepal	
Chad	Ivory Coast	Niger	Upper Volta
Dahomey	Kenya	Pakistan	Yemen Arab Republic

[9]Arnold Rorholt, *Pre-Disaster Planning and Organization of Disaster Assistance*, paper prepared for and distributed by the League of Red Cross Societies, Geneva, 1974, p. 2.

21

THREE

Disasters of the 1980s

There are several reasons to conclude that the severity of disasters, in terms of their human effects, will increase over the coming 15 to 20 years. World population will of course grow and will increase comparatively more in the less developed countries (LDCs). What is not often appreciated is that even within the group of LDCs, the least developed, worst-disaster-prone countries have a yet higher population growth rate, so that the 1980s will see many more poor, hungry, or near-hungry people crowded into the very areas of the globe where, historically, disasters have occurred most often (see Table 5).

TABLE 5
Population in Millions, UN Medium Variant Estimates

Region	1975	1990	Increase (Percent)
World totals	3,967	5,279	33
More developed countries	1,132	1,278	11
Less developed countries	2,835	4,001	41
Group X	812	1,181	46

SOURCE: United Nations, "World Population Prospects, 1970–2000, as Assessed in 1973," in Georges Tapinos (tr. Edward Morse), *The World in the 1980s: Demographic Perspectives,* Council on Foreign Relations, New York, 1976. (Mimeographed.)

Group X in Table 5 is composed of 10 countries: India, Bangladesh, Pakistan, Ethiopia, and the six countries in the Sahel hardest hit by the 1968–1973 drought. These countries lie almost entirely within ecologically overstressed areas that are now in a more or less permanent state of emergency. The natural population growth rates of the regions of the world most susceptible to disasters will not change significantly between 1975 and 1990, except in Africa, where they will increase (see Table 6).

Georges Tapinos has argued that the short-term UN predictions are quite reliable:

In effect, the demographic situation is like the picture of a car traveling at a certain speed, and which an observer placed along the road looks at, at a given point in time. The demographic situation as we have described it in 1990 results from an ineluctable evolutionary trail which no demographic policy, however coercive, can change in so brief a period of time.[10]

That may be true with respect to demographic policies or to changes in crude birthrates which can be controlled by national population policies. However, population growth rates already underwent sudden fluctuations in the early 1970s, when populations were reduced by several hundred thousand in a very few hours (East Pakistan, 1970) or a very few months (Burundi, 1972, and Ethiopia, 1973).[11]

TABLE 6
Evolution of the Natural Growth Rates in South Asia, Latin America, and Africa

Region	1970–1975	1975–1980	1980–1985	1985–1990
South Asia	2.53	2.61	2.56	2.41
Latin America	2.77	2.78	2.75	2.66
Africa	2.65	2.77	2.86	2.88

SOURCE: United Nations, "World Population Prospects, 1970–2000, as Assessed in 1973," in Georges Tapinos (tr. Edward Morse), *The World in the 1980s: Demographic Perspectives*, Council on Foreign Relations, New York, 1976. (Mimeographed.)

[10]Georges Tapinos (tr. Edward Morse), *The World in the 1980s: Demographic Perspectives*, Council on Foreign Relations, New York, 1976. This is a draft discussion paper that will be revised in 1977.

[11]See Morris Davis, *Civil Wars and the Politics of International Relief,* Praeger, chaps. 2 and 3, New York, 1975, for the figures on East Pakistan and Burundi.

Disasters of this magnitude will probably be frequent in the 1980s; they will be as fully political as the disasters of the 1970s; and their political ramifications will be as significant. The governments (in particular, the major intelligence agencies) of both the United States and the Soviet Union have devoted considerable time and effort to projecting the dimensions and political ramifications of future natural disasters. Several recent studies by the CIA, for example, have concluded that future natural disasters will cause wide-scale political instability and conflict.[12]

Population increase is by no means the only reason for the approaching megadisasters. Another is the curtailment in some countries of urgent development programs, which has led to a reversal of the social development process—fewer being educated, vaccinated, trained, well fed, etc., than in the preceding years, all in the heralded second UN "Development Decade." Energy costs, food export prices, air and water erosion of the land, political crises in capital cities, ethnic conflicts in rural areas are but a few of the factors halting, and in some cases reversing, the economic and social development process in several of the world's poorest, most populous areas. As a result, *a substantial number of countries (essentially the 44 listed in Table 4) have become so marginal economically that they simply cannot afford to have a disaster. They have no defenses left.*

Another variable—the weather—could well hasten the disasters these countries cannot afford to have. The CIA predicts future global climatic changes that will shorten growing seasons over most of the earth and cause severe droughts and floods in many sections. The result, according to its report, will be famine and starvation on a scale yet unknown and a period in which "the politics of food will become the central issue of every government."[13]

A February 1975 Rockefeller Foundation report on the Bellagio conference on "Climate Change, Food Production and Interstate Conflict" drew strikingly similar conclusions. The conference, which

---

The Ethiopian government confirmed officially, in 1976, a final death toll of over 200,000 persons for the 1973 famine in that country.

[12]Since 1972, the CIA has published at least three studies on this subject—one of which is cited in Chapter 2. For evidence of Soviet official concern and attention to the subject, see *Famine and People: The Politics of Food*, Background Brief 67, Institute of Applied Semantics (a subsidiary of the Universal Bureau of Applied Languages), Washington, D.C., 1967.

[13]*A Study of Climatological Research as It Pertains to Intelligence Problems*, August 1974, op. cit., p. 3.

brought together experts on climatology and food production, agreed that "weather had re-emerged as a major destabilizer of the world economic system." The chairman of the conference noted in the report that "the tragedy in the Sahel needs no underlining. If drought on such a scale were to touch the densely populated countries of southern Asia it would confront the world with a catastrophe beyond imagining. Climatologically this is within the bounds of possibility." The report points out that the climatological anomalies of the early 1970s were in fact relatively minor and limited in scope. They produced the dramatic adverse human effects because of where and when they occurred.

Whether or not one accepts such projections of a cataclysmic future, there can be little doubt that a number of regions of the world have moved to a position where *any* interruption in optimal rainfall and weather patterns will in the future cause local disaster situations of a very large magnitude. The Ethiopian famine of 1973 is a good example of this—almost a quarter of a million deaths were caused by a relatively minor break in normal rainfall over a period of two or three growing seasons.

A new type of disaster that does not conveniently fit any of these categories also seems to be developing—the *technological* disaster. An example is the mass poisoning that occurred in Morocco in 1959. Some 10,000 people were killed, blinded, or otherwise permanently affected when cooking oil mixed with motor oil was eaten by ill-informed peasants. The CSLP report on short-lived phenomena cited earlier also indicates that certain other kinds of technological disasters are increasing (see Table 7).

TABLE 7

Types and Number of Events Reported by the Center for Short-Lived Phenomena, 1968–1974

Pollution Events	1968	1969	1970	1971	1972	1973	1974	Total
Major oil spills	7	15	14	16	20	23	48	143
Other pollution events	0	3	6	4	7	21	28	69

SOURCE: *1974 Annual Report, Center for Short-Lived Phenomena,* Cambridge, Mass., 1976.

In view of the population projections described previously, and the confluence in the 1980s of food, economic, environmental, technological, and political problems, I would envision the following situation developing:

- *Sudden disasters will likely be more frequent and severe.* Their frequency will increase because environmental problems will cause floods and landslides where previously soil would have resisted water, and population concentrations may turn "fires" that would have been containable into situations requiring international aid. The effects of sudden disasters, including earthquakes, cyclones, and volcanoes, will be more severe because they will occur in areas that are more densely populated than they were previously.

- *Slow-developing disasters will likely cause dying on a scale previously known only in wartime, in fact for many of the same reasons that deaths occur during wars.* Very simply, mankind will be preoccupied with conflicts, energy shortages, economic problems, and so on. The sheer number and geographic spread of people suffering from undernutrition will increase the probability that temporary changes in rainfall patterns will cause severe famines. Chronic undernutrition and malnutrition will in turn raise the specter of epidemics, many involving diseases supposedly eliminated from a given area—such as the smallpox and cholera that spread through Ethiopia in 1973.

- *Virtually all of the long- and short-term factors will contribute to political instability and result in both internal and international conflicts.* One of the chapter headings in the apocalyptic book *Famine, 1975* asked the question, "In Times of Stress, Do People Retrogress?"[14] In the 1980s the grim likelihood is that, as the Paddocks indicate, disasters will spur ignorance, rigid ethnicity, urban alienation, defensive nationalism, and other human problems leading to violence. The interaction between disasters and conflicts may become cyclical and mutually reinforcing.

These factors may have such adverse consequences that disaster relief coordination activities will be more prominent than efforts at disaster prevention in the next two decades. Basically, the fundamental concept of disaster prevention is that properly warned, properly prepared, properly situated and housed, mankind can mitigate the worst effects of natural (and, to some extent, human-caused) occurrences that otherwise would involve great loss of life and suffering. My fear is that the multiple crises we will have to face in the next 15 years may distract us from preventive measures.

[14]William Paddock and Paul Paddock, *Famine, 1975*, Little, Brown, Boston, 1967, chap. 4.

FOUR

The Present System

The present international disaster relief system is composed of four major elements:

- *The United Nations*, many of whose technical and programming agencies provide funds, relief goods, equipment in kind, and technical assistance. The UN agencies are involved in almost all disasters requiring international assistance but may provide only a small proportion of assistance in any given relief operation.

- *Private organizations,* which both raise their own funds for emergency operations and act as a conduit for government and (occasionally) UN contributions. Unlike the UN or other governments, the private agencies may have a ''franchise'' (branch organization) in the disaster-afflicted country, composed of its citizens. Such is the case with the Red Cross and with many church organizations.

- *Donor governments*, which often provide the majority of the total assistance, although some of their aid is channeled through the UN or private agencies.

- *The international media*, which carry the major burden for mobilizing world concern for disaster organizations. The press is often the first to acknowledge a disaster situation and often provides the only evaluation made of relief operations during and after the event.

This system is complex if not chaotic: as the UNDRO list indicates, disasters that require international assistance occur every two to three weeks; the major relief organizations must deal with several operations at one time; and the hundreds of organizations that do some relief work spend several hundred million dollars annually. In fact, it is a non-system, a series of ad hoc responses to the differing circumstances and geographical locations of each major emergency. Rorholt describes the usual relief operations as:

a kind of "mass assault" on a disaster-struck country by a number of governments, intergovernmental and non-governmental agencies, each one trying to meet a real or supposed need, by sending personnel, equipment and supplies which do not meet the needs of the disaster victims. The work is done, after a fashion, but at the cost of delays, lack of coordination and efficiency with gaps and duplication of effort, and at high expense—all of which creates justified criticism.[15]

Perhaps the fundamental management problem faced by many disaster relief agencies is their administrations' refusal until recently to institutionalize emergency assistance. Until 1975, the Food and Agriculturel Organization (FAO), the World Food Programme (WFP), and the World Health Organization (WHO) did not have separate, specialized bureaus to handle their constant involvements in relief operations, and the United Nations Children's Fund (UNICEF) struggled in 1974 to manage over $30 million in emergency programs with an "emergency desk" staffed by one professional and two "general service" (clerical) staff members. UNICEF's relief projects are staffed almost entirely by persons temporarily detached from other, "regular" programs. One of the adverse effects of this general approach is that most relief operations must be training exercises for relatively inexperienced personnel. This is generally true from the top to the bottom, from administrators to field operatives.[16] Fortunately, however, the size and frequency of recent major disasters, along with the amount of money dispersed, have begun to convince most of the major agencies to upgrade their relief capacities.

While the relief organizations themselves have often attributed their

[15]Rorholt, *Pre-Disaster Planning*, p. 5.
[16]Lawrence Burley, "Disaster Relief Administration in the Third World," *International Development Review*, 1973/1, p. 10.

ad hoc approach to a lack of staff and time or to a desire to cut administrative costs, other observers have noted the lack of systematic evaluation—the simple inability to distill and apply the experiences of previous relief operations. Part of the reason for this relates to the manner in which these organizations raise their funds. It has been argued—with justification—that most information produced by international relief organizations about their work is designed to enhance the agencies' reputations, to satisfy past funding sources, and to elicit future support. These "self-portraits" usually reflect the ideas of the agencies' home offices rather than the views of their personnel in the field.[17]

Another natural concomitant of the ad hoc approach has been a general lack of practical coordination among the relief agencies during the operations themselves. A certain amount of improvisation will, of course, be necessary in major relief operations, for each disaster presents a different set of circumstances—in terms of causes of death and suffering, mixes of relief needs and transportation problems, and the organizational capabilities of each affected developing country's government. Nevertheless, independent observers of the "system" are virtually unanimous in their condemnation of the chaos of international relief and in their advocacy of coordination. For this reason the need for coordination has been a recurring theme in relief circles for several years. The following survey of the major organizational components of the international disaster relief system begins with a discussion of the most important recent development aimed at strengthening coordination.

THE UNITED NATIONS

In December 1971, the UN General Assembly adopted Resolution 2816 (see Appendix B), creating the Office of the United Nations Disaster Relief Coordinator (UNDRO). The Office was to be "a focal point in the United Nations system for disaster relief matters." The resolution mandated two primary functions for UNDRO:

1) To mobilize, direct, and coordinate external aid provided (by the UN system) in response to a request from a disaster-stricken state;

[17]Morris Davis, "Some Political Dimensions of International Relief: Two Cases," *International Organization,* vol. 28, no. 1 (Winter 1974), pp. 127–128. See also Jean Mayer, "Coping with Famine," *Foreign Affairs,* vol. 53, no. 1, October 1974.

2) To promote the study, prevention, control, and prediction of natural disasters, including the collection and dissemination of information concerning technological developments, and as part of this latter function, to assist in providing advice to governments on predisaster planning.

Recognizing that the Coordinator in Geneva would need status within the UN system to deal with the gaggle of specialized agencies involved with disasters, the resolution created the position of Coordinator at the level of Undersecretary-General, reporting directly to the Secretary-General.

Nevertheless, UNDRO was "coordinative" in name only. Even as a central UN information exchange on disasters, UNDRO was severely hampered; although Resolution 2816 gave it a mandate of sorts, it did not provide adequate staff. During its first three years (1972–1975), the Office struggled to enlarge its staff from two to six. To be sure, the lack of staff and funds was not the only problem UNDRO faced. The Office, small as it was, suffered from confused internal lines of authority.[18] The infamous UN personnel system, with its politics and internal quota systems, severely limited the ability of the Coordinator to assemble a qualified staff. Perhaps most important, UNDRO's mandate in Resolution 2816 had been left purposely vague in several respects, in order to lessen the expected UN interagency jealousies and resistance to being "coordinated." Thus, the Office faced considerable competition from other UN agencies for relief fund raising and often did not have the full cooperation of other UN agency field staff, through whom it had to work in the field.[19]

Finally, UNDRO's working relationships with the Red Cross were less than ideal. The final report of a three-year reappraisal of the role of the Red Cross is extremely candid on this point:

While Red Cross enjoys a close working relationship with certain UN agencies such as WHO and UNICEF, this is not true for UNDRO. The mutual reluctance of UNDRO and the League to cooperate is particularly striking given the

[18]These problems are detailed in an internal report to the UN Disaster Relief Coordinator submitted by the UN Bureau of Administrative Services in August 1974.

[19]For a candid discussion of the problem of cooperation from the field, see the *Report of the Panel of Consultants on Strengthening the Relief and Coordination Capacity of the Office of the United Nations Disaster Relief Coordinator (UNDRO)*, submitted to the Coordinator in February 1975, p. 8.

similarity of their mandates. . . . Given the pressures now building in the international community for cooperation among disaster assistance organizations this relationship now seems unjustifiable, whatever factors led to it in the past.[20]

The League has vigorously protested against this part of the report, and there is every reason to believe that the problem is being resolved, as several joint endeavors between the League and UNDRO have recently begun.

When the General Assembly's Twenty-Ninth Session opened in September 1974, U.S. Secretary of State Kissinger called for the strengthening of UNDRO. This set in train a long succession of events that led to a dramatic expansion of the Office's staff and funding in mid-1975. Beyond adding equipment and administrative expenses, UNDRO increased its staff from 11 to 46. Although this expansion is an interim arrangement funded by bilateral donors (notably the United States), the increased costs of UNDRO's operation probably will be incorporated into the regular 1977 UN budget when the bilateral funding is terminated.

The expansion has not solved all of UNDRO's problems, but it has made the organization a solid base to build on in the future. A May 1976 report to the U.S. Congress by the General Accounting Office (GAO) described the new UNDRO as "young and basically underdeveloped" and still lacking the authority and resource base to perform the coordinative functions required by the present, far-flung international disaster relief system. The title of the GAO report reflects both UNDRO's limitations and its potential—it was called *Need for an International Disaster Relief Agency*.

In spite of the agency's troubles, the idea of UNDRO as an information clearinghouse has always had support from its sister UN agencies and indeed from the entire international disaster relief system. All parties, moreover, seem to be gradually accepting its coordinating function, and UNDRO's expansion will certainly give it the wherewithal to play this role. However, there remains considerable disagreement within the system about UNDRO's *operational* role in disaster relief and the nature of its responsibilities for disaster preparedness and disaster prevention.

[20]Donald D. Tansley, *Final Report: An Agenda for Red Cross*, Joint Committee for the Reappraisal of the Red Cross, Geneva, 1975, p. 79.

The creation of UNDRO in 1971 altered somewhat the traditional relief roles of the other UN agencies—notably that of the central UN development agency, the United Nations Development Programme (UNDP). The UNDP Resident Representative was generally the senior UN person in each developing country (except where other agencies had regional offices), but tended to be ineffective in disaster situations. Disasters interfered with the UNDP planning process and created human problems which, in any event, UNICEF and some of the specialized agencies were better equipped to handle. So UNDP, normally the programming and planning agency for all UN economic development assistance, was often uncertain about the extent to which the coordination of "charity operations" fell within its mandate.

When General Assembly Resolution 2816 created UNDRO it did not specify any particular role for UNDP in disaster operations, nor did it spell out any working relationship between the UNDP Resident Representative in a disaster-affected country and the Office of the UN Disaster Relief Coordinator in Geneva. In the last two or three years, however, UNDP and UNDRO have drawn up formal agreements making the Resident Representative the local "representative," or agent, of the Coordinator during relief operations. In general, this arrangement has worked satisfactorily.

Other UN agencies with supplementary disaster relief functions, whose operations are still in the process of being coordinated with UNDRO's, are the following:

The United Nations Children's Fund (UNICEF), which concentrates on the special needs of children and young mothers in disasters. In practice, UNICEF often programs, purchases, ships, and assists with the internal distribution of a wide range of supplies (including food) and equipment needed for relief operations generally. The Fund's broad mandate (what does not affect children?) and its jealously guarded fund-raising capacities give it a flexibility that is unique among UN agencies. It is often the only UN agency in-country with a complete supply operation (for its regular assistance programs) intact at the time of a disaster. Another unique feature is its public information resources, which have made UNICEF the best-known UN agency and are often used to inform the public of the grim details of a disaster.

The Food and Agriculture Organization (FAO), which approves emergency food aid provided through the facilities of its subsidiary organization, the World Food Programme (WFP). When a disaster occurs, FAO's Country Representative and in-country personnel advise the UNDP Resident Representative on emergency operations matters pertaining to food and nutrition and on the agricultural reconstruction and rehabilitation phase of an emergency, usually in a technical advisory capacity to the local government.

The World Food Programme (WFP), which in addition to providing emergency food may also assist a government in receiving and distributing it. WFP's advice to the UNDP Resident Representative and the local government on emergency food needs created by a disaster is particularly important.

The World Health Organization (WHO), which advises the UNDP Resident Representative and the local government on the public health implications of a disaster, approves the furnishing of and (occasionally) purchases and ships medical equipment and supplies for UN-assisted relief operations. WHO field teams and advisers may assist with emergency vaccination and treatment measures as well.

The United Nations High Commission for Refugees (UNHCR), which plays a major role among UN agencies, sometimes the only one, in disasters of human origin, such as international and internal conflicts. UNHCR focuses primarily on meeting the short- and medium-term needs (prior to resettlement) of refugees who have fled across national borders. Like UNICEF, UNHCR can raise some of its own funds by direct solicitation.

Other UN agencies are also involved in emergency relief, though not necessarily in the postdisaster activities themselves. The *International Telecommunications Union (ITU)* has helped to establish some of the communications links that assist UNDRO and other UN agency headquarters to assess the situation and coordinate operations after a disaster. The *World Meteorological Organization (WMO)*, through its World Weather Watch program, provides information that helps to mitigate the worst effects of many natural disasters. Its cooperation in regional typhoon warnings in South and East Asia and the Western Pacific is particularly important. The *United Nations Environmental Programme (UNEP)* and the *UN Center for Housing, Building and Planning* cooperate with UNDRO in the disaster prevention field, as does the *United Nations Educational, Scientific and Cultural Organization (UNESCO)*.

How these various organizations work together in the field during a disaster relief operation varies from case to case—even in the post-UNDRO period and up to the present. In many instances, as with UNICEF activities in the Nigerian/Biafran War, the relief initiative was taken by individual UN agencies, which then informally became the UN

35

focal points in relief operations. At other times, as with the FAO in the Sahelian drought, the Secretary-General appointed one agency to be the special, one-time focal point. And occasionally a special UN agency has been created: in the 1970–1972 Pakistan/Bangladesh flood and war emergency, the UN Relief Office/Dacca (UNDROD—later UNROB for UN Relief Office Bangladesh) coordinated the various UN activities.

PRIVATE ORGANIZATIONS

Private agencies generally provide a relatively small portion of the assistance in a given disaster, but for several reasons they form an important part of the international relief picture. First, they tend to be in action before UN agencies or governments. The church groups in particular often have people and resources already in a country when there is a sudden natural disaster or outbreak of violence; they can be in the field with their assistance while foreign ministries and the UN organizations are still cabling each other to find out what *really* happened. Second, the private groups can often provide assistance (unofficially) in places where and at times when, for political reasons, the official organizations cannot. This occurred in Biafra in 1969–1970 and in Burundi in 1972. And third, several of the private relief organizations have a flexibility to provide different types of relief matched by few, if any, of the official groups.

Since most private groups do their own fund raising, sustained global cooperation among them has been slow in developing. Money and gifts in kind come from individuals, companies, and donor governments that expect that their contributions will be used for a specific purpose or disaster by the particular relief organization to whom the contribution was made. Joint operations and projects appear to contributors to muddy the water of accountability.

However, this situation changed in 1972 when an informal committee of five of the major relief agencies was set up in Geneva. Since its inception, this group—known as the Steering Committee—has consulted regularly, sometimes daily, on ongoing disaster relief operations. Members of the group are the Oxford Committee for Famine Relief (OXFAM), Catholic Relief Services (CRS), the World Council of Churches (WCC), the Lutheran World Federation (LWF), and the League of Red Cross Societies.

The Steering Committee has achieved impressive results quietly and without minutes, agendas, or even letterhead stationery. Using office space provided by the League and one full-time staff member, it has become an important central coordinating body for private relief activities worldwide. Besides consulting regularly on relief operations in progress, the Steering Committee has collated and summarized all existing national disaster plans, drawn up country profiles of disaster-related information on developing nations, and completed an inventory of worldwide university faculties doing disaster-related research and teaching. At the present time, the Steering Committee is completing work on an operational handbook intended for use by field representatives of the private relief organizations.

Throughout its short history, the Steering Committee has resisted the temptation to become a formal organization and to expand its membership to other private relief agencies, on the quite plausible theory that the effectiveness of groups like itself is inversely proportional to their size and the number of things they commit to paper.

The Steering Committee's influence reaches well beyond Geneva; though it has only five members, they themselves are hubs of relief networks. The League, OXFAM, and the church groups (particularly the World Council) all act as information centers for their members—who are potential donors—immediately after a disaster occurs.

Coordination between the Steering Committee and UNDRO is informal. During a relief operation, phone contact is more or less regularly maintained between UNDRO and the major Steering Committee members' offices in Geneva. UNDRO cables its situation reports, as well, to the Steering Committee and to many other private organizations around the world.

The Steering Committee has also provided a forum for information exchange for a broader spectrum of relief agencies—virtually all of those represented in Geneva. Once a month, approximately 15 to 25 of the UN organizations and private relief groups meet in the League's Geneva headquarters to exchange information about the extent of damage, number of victims, assessed needs, relief provided, transport problems, etc., associated with current disaster situations. Again, no fixed agenda is set, and only the barest of minutes are prepared.

The Red Cross is a unique part of the structure of international relief and deserves more elaborate examination here. In a sense, it does not fit within this section, for it is not really a private organization; in fact, it is not an organization at all. The Red Cross is a movement of individuals who provide their services and funds, organizations that serve its purposes, and even governments that sit in its governing councils and support its activities financially.

The movement is composed of three distinct elements:

- *The International Committee of the Red Cross (ICRC)* is the parent organization. Founded in 1863 in Geneva, the ICRC is often referred to as the guardian of the Red Cross principles. Its primary purpose is the "protection," through implementation of international law and humanitarian principles, of war wounded, prisoners of war, and civilians, in both international and internal conflicts. But it can also, in these situations, assume responsibility for major relief operations. Increasingly in recent years, the ICRC has concerned itself with political detainees.

- Soon after the ICRC was founded, governments were invited to form *national Red Cross organizations*; since that time, 122 countries have done so. These "societies," as they are called, constitute the second element of the movement. Instead of protection, they concentrate on relief, public health, and welfare; some of them have broadened their fields of activity to encompass virtually the entire population of their respective countries.

- In 1919, about 60 national Red Cross societies formed a federation, the *League of Red Cross Societies*, which is the third element of the International Red Cross. The secretariat, or headquarters, of this federation has begun to assume certain international responsibilities and functions on its own in addition to (though not necessarily independent from) the concerns of the individual national Red Cross societies. The relief coordination activities described above are examples of this.

Policy direction for the various entities of the Red Cross is achieved at an international conference, usually convened every four years, which involves all Red Cross agencies including the 122 national societies and representatives of their respective national governments. In the intervals between international conferences, intra–Red Cross policy matters are dealt with on a regular basis by a joint policy coordination committee, created to carry out a series of bilateral agreements between the League and the ICRC. This coordination committee decides such matters as

38

which Red Cross element will have prime responsibility for a relief operation and whether a joint action might be appropriate.

Since these private agencies do work more or less in concert with each other, they have been emphasized as a central part of the existing structure of nongovernmental international relief. Obviously, there is not space here to run the gamut of all relief agencies, donor country by donor country. In addition to the member organizations of the Steering Committee, hundreds of private groups are involved in disaster relief. Some, such as CARE and the "Save the Children" organizations, operate more or less independently. Others, such as Church World Service and Caritas Internationalis, are linked to one of the Steering Committee member organizations.

The UN and private organization focal points in Geneva cannot function effectively without smooth operations elsewhere. Neither funding sources nor the disaster victims are generally in Switzerland. Coordination is therefore necessary as well in both donor countries and the disaster areas themselves.

Currently, about 20 percent of the 40 to 50 disaster-prone developing countries have some sort of permanent disaster committee arrangement for the various private agencies that are already present and can assist in an emergency. In most instances, such committees were established under strong government leadership as part of a national disaster relief organization during or after a major disaster in which the importance of preplanning and cooperation was amply demonstrated. It is difficult to exaggerate the importance of a strong national disaster relief organization in the midst of the confusion and trauma of a major disaster. That there has not before now been a global program of "preparedness" assistance to virtually all disaster-prone countries reflects adversely on both the national governments (for not making preparedness a priority in their development assistance plans) and the major development assistance agencies themselves (for not encouraging the governments to do so).

A third type or level of coordination exists in those industrialized nations where large numbers of private groups provide international disaster assistance. Several governments—such as those of Great Britain, Australia, Canada, and Switzerland—have encouraged the formation of national coordinating groups to lessen competition and duplication. The oldest and best known of these is the Disaster Emergency Committee in Great Britain.

39

DONOR GOVERNMENTS

A number of development or foreign aid ministries in industrialized countries have recently formed special bureaus to deal with disaster aid. Great Britain, France, Sweden, Australia, New Zealand, Canada, and the United States now have such offices. The USAID Office of Foreign Disaster Assistance is the largest and oldest of these and really developed the international disaster relief "operations room" concept.

While these "bilateral" offices have long been the single largest source of disaster relief (almost invariably larger than the UN or private sectors), they have tended until recently to work in relative isolation from each other. That is, they made policy decisions internally regarding the size of contributions to a given disaster and the channel to be used. Occasionally, contributions were made through the UN, the European Economic Community (EEC) (in the case of European donor governments), or one of several of the private relief agencies—a favorite being the Red Cross network. More often, bilateral agencies contributed directly to the disaster-affected country in order to achieve maximum political impact.

Within the last two years, however, there has been a noticeable trend toward regular or even automatic contributions through UNDRO. The Netherlands, for example, has an unwritten but relatively firm understanding with UNDRO to make up to a million florins immediately available upon the UN Disaster Relief Coordinator's certification that a disaster of a certain size has in fact occurred. The details of expenditures and reports on final use are left to UNDRO, and a final accounting may be made after the operation is completed. This method helps considerably to systematize overall relief operations; since UNDRO is well placed to know what all (or most) other contributors are providing daily, wasteful duplication can generally be avoided.

THE INTERNATIONAL MEDIA

The fourth major element in the international disaster relief system is the international print and broadcast media. The impact of the international media in recent major natural disasters can scarcely be exaggerated. The levels of contributions, for one thing, are largely determined by the "play" given a particular disaster in the media.[21] The Federal Republic of Germany provided over \$10 million to the Ethiopian famine operations, largely because of a year-long campaign on the subject mounted by *Stern* magazine.

Critical accounts, too, serve their purpose. For reasons already noted, the organizations that compose the international disaster relief system are largely incapable of evaluating their own performance. In the later stages of most relief operations, the print and broadcast media ferret out examples of duplication and inefficiency. One informed observer has maintained that it is such coverage, together with the vivid portrayals of suffering and dying, that has been largely responsible for the recent serious efforts to make emergency relief more systematic.[22]

There is a final, most important role that the media play. Traditional diplomacy—practiced by embassies and UN representatives in a disaster-stricken country—has repeatedly proved unable to remove the political barriers to the commencement and/or efficient operation of relief programs. For their own reasons, governments have sometimes denied the existence of a disaster or delayed and diverted relief from the most needy victims. Governments have, for example, decided that the acknowledgment of cholera would discourage tourists or frighten agricultural export markets.

National sovereignty—or an interpretation of it which has in fact been shaped by the narrow, self-perceived interests of a small group of politicians—has in these ways frequently caused thousands of needless deaths and greatly increased the impact of disasters on the "normal" development process. Confronted with such barriers, the humanitarian principles of relief organizations, professional codes of ethics, and the individual courage and conscience of senior diplomats and international organization representatives can disappear in the twinkling of an eye. At such times, the only remaining hope for relief rests with the pressure the media can exert on the "leaders" concerned. It is doubtful that there ever would have been an Ethiopian famine operation had the press not intervened. If, as many believe, the size and severity of disasters will continue to overwhelm the international relief system, it is unlikely that the importance of the media within that system will diminish.

[21]Holdsworth, *Red Cross*, p. 18.

[22]Roger Morris, *Disaster in the Desert*, Carnegie Endowment for International Peace, Washington, D.C., 1974, p. 64.

FIVE

Reorganizing Relief

Much has been done, in the last few years, to begin to bring order to the traditionally ad hoc process of international disaster relief. And there are many signs of more fundamental reforms to come:

- UNDRO has been greatly expanded and its operations professionalized.
- The Red Cross movement, which for years had been developing a wide range of programs, has recently completed a study of its capacity that recommends that it limit its basic future role to protection and assistance in emergencies.
- UNDP is assessing its capacities to help developing countries prepare for disasters.
- The United States government, under a contract with the National Academy of Sciences, is examining the prospects and priorities for applying modern technology to disaster relief.
- The United Nations Association of the United States is studying the organizational and political problems involved in major international emergencies.

This is but a sample of the growing interest and activity in disaster relief reform, suggesting that fundamental changes are possible—indeed, likely—in the next decade. Ideally, comprehensive reorganization of the entire multilateral development assistance system would be the context for disaster relief reform, for the two activities should be seen as inseparable. It is possible that a major disaster, involving widespread suffering and turmoil, might instigate reforms reaching far beyond the disaster relief system. But prescriptions for specific reform ought not to depend on the assumption of broad progress. The pages that follow, therefore, concentrate on what in my view is likely to be done and should be done to improve and harmonize the international disaster relief system in a context not unlike today's.

PROGNOSIS

Changes in the international disaster relief system are likely to occur in three major areas: (1) coordination, (2) the application of modern technology, and (3) disaster preparedness.

Coordination

The United Nations system—UNDRO, UNDP, and the relevant technical agencies—will gradually begin to predominate in the coordination of major relief operations. While governments and private organizations may continue to provide most of the money, funds will increasingly be channeled through and administered by the UN.

There are several reasons to think this trend is likely. Governments of developing countries are steadily increasing their own capacities to manage the complex logistics of relief operations, and the UN's contacts with them on development assistance matters are far more extensive than are those of either the private organizations or other governments. Moreover, the UN specialized agencies in health, agriculture, community development, nutrition, and other disaster-related areas generally have more technical resources in-country than do other elements of the development assistance/disaster relief establishment. Finally, the UN aegis for relief—its visible presence in highly publicized, politically traumatized relief situations—is generally more acceptable to the governments of developing countries.

There are exceptions to these general points, of course, especially in Third World regions where industrialized states maintain strong traditional relationships, such as France does in parts of Africa or the United States does in certain countries of Latin America. But on the whole, the sheer weight of the UN's technical resources and experience together with its almost universal prestige recommend it for international pre-eminence in disaster relief—at least in the operational phase.

Within the UN, UNDRO will consolidate its function as an information clearinghouse, with the Red Cross, the World Council of Churches, and others possibly participating directly in staffing and funding. Such a reform would create, in other words, a genuinely "joint" operations room. In the immediate aftermath of disasters, the Red Cross and UNDRO would jointly coordinate missions to advise and assist the local government and Red Cross society.

Donor governments will increasingly use UNDRO as a funding channel, and direct bilateral relief aid will correspondingly diminish. In turn, UNDRO will become more professionalized; with its increased staff and telecommunications equipment, it will perform an accepted, automatic UN service to donors and governments of developing countries in times of disaster.

As national relief organizations are formed and begin to function in more and more developing countries, they will increasingly assume direct responsibility for the local operational matters, ranging from damage assessment to accounting and reporting as the relief phase ends. As this consolidation occurs, operational roles of all international assistance agencies will diminish commensurately, or at least they will stop at the borders of the disaster-affected country.

One noteworthy exception may be the League of Red Cross Societies, whose assets as a relief organization stem directly from the strength of its various national affiliates. While national Red Cross societies are only as strong as the local governments permit them to be, it appears likely that more and more countries will make them the keystone of national disaster plans. Governments need trained local people if they are to manage and control a modern relief operation. The Red Cross movement's independence from external political manipulation, its national identity through the local society, and the training and support services (emphasizing community self-help and voluntarism) available from the League will all strongly influence governments of developing countries to strengthen their national Red Cross organizations.

Application of Modern Technology

Modern technology can make relief operations more efficient and sys-tematized. What is perhaps less obvious is that its application can also provide early warning that can substantially reduce the physical,

45

psychological, and political costs of disasters. Satellite photographs, data-processed field surveys, and other techniques can provide early information about slow-developing disasters. Modern transport and telecommunications can speed relief to areas otherwise not accessible or to accessible areas in less time. Thus, technological capabilities can help governments and organizations to mount their relief operations *before* they are accused of delay and incompetence or of causing needless deaths. In this respect, early-warning systems for epidemics and famines are particularly important.

But before any such early-warning system can be developed, national governments must agree to cooperate with relief organizations in developing mechanisms for automatic sharing of information on crop projections, nutrition status, communicable disease incidence, and other technical matters that would constitute the guts of the system. A good start has already been made with the WMO's World Weather Watch project and the Asia and Western Pacific typhoon-warning system, in which WMO also participates. Diplomatic conferences and formal instruments will be necessary if such sharing of information is to be automatic. The need for this is now so obvious that national governments are likely to try very soon to achieve the necessary agreements.

However, a significant centralization of such technical capabilities is unlikely to happen soon. Donor governments are unlikely to fund a centralized relief force that would reduce the visibility of their own contributions. And recipient governments will not be eager to institutionalize a potential threat to their national sovereignty. For these reasons, particular organizations are likely to put technology to use separately—USAID in telecommunications and transport, FAO in use of satellite photographs for crop projections, UNDRO in communications and data processing, etc.—rather than as components of an integrated system.

In order to fulfill more effectively its coordinating role, UNDRO must be thoroughly aware of these developments. While UNDRO's staff will become increasingly specialized as a result, centralized control—however attractive a managerial concept—is still politically unlikely.

Disaster Preparedness

Disaster preparedness will be the fastest-growing activity in the relief field for the next few years. The UN and the League will attempt jointly and systematically to assist governments in virtually all disaster-prone countries to develop national disaster plans and organizations, including complementary governmental and national Red Cross capacities. These efforts will be funded by bilateral development aid ministries, the World Bank, UNDP, and the regional development banks as an integral part of national development plans and on a scale far exceeding the present case. Included in the national plans will be such matters as:

- Laws establishing the national disaster relief organization and providing its legal authority
- The organization plan of the national relief office
- Cooperation among the national government, the Red Cross, community officials, and relief organizations
- Means of communication with UNDRO
- Plans for assessment surveys
- Emergency health services
- Provision and storage of shelter, food, and clothing
- Internal supply and transportation
- Internal communication
- Mobile disaster relief units (depending upon existing infrastructures)
- Central receipt and handling of international assistance
- Customs arrangements for duty-free entry of international assistance goods
- Tracing services
- Evacuation plans
- Finance and accounting
- Public information
- Monitoring and reporting
- Personnel

Early activity and progress in this field seem very likely, partly because so many least-developed, ''Fourth World'' countries have had a devastating disaster within the last four years. More often than not, their national governments have been tried and convicted in the international press of backwardness, callousness, inefficiency, and worse. Many have determined not to relive that experience and are now seeking the funds and technical assistance with which to prepare themselves for the next disaster.

PRESCRIPTION

Beyond what appears *likely* to happen in the international disaster relief system, there are a number of things that I think *should* happen.

Coordination

A working global disaster relief system must reconcile a basic paradox: to obtain maximum public support, its many components must remain responsive to their own special constituencies; yet to carry out relief operations effectively, these components—and their potentially conflicting interests—must be melded into a whole whose elements know what one another is doing.

As national disaster relief organizations are established in more and more countries, they will—and should—become the information, coordination, funding, and administrative focal points for all emergency relief operations. The patterns will vary from country to country, however. Some LDCs that have not yet had a serious disaster may continue to see disaster preparedness as a bit of a luxury, given other urgent development priorities. When a disaster does occur in these countries, a loose combination of voluntary agencies and confused personnel will continue to administer relief operations as they try to get assistance from UNDRO and other international sources.

Whatever the national relief capabilities may be, there should be one and only one global focal point for international disaster relief—and that should be UNDRO in Geneva. In their desire for administrative neatness, some observers would go beyond this and recommend an in-country operational responsibility for UNDRO.[23] This is neither practical nor desirable, for two reasons: (1) foreign personnel would be learning the "lay of the land" while the logistics problems piled up, and (2) national governments would not in most instances appreciate or allow in-country relief administrators in any event.

[23]Report to the Congress by the Comptroller General of the United States (General Accounting Office), *Need for an International Disaster Relief Agency*, Department of State, AID, May 5, 1976, p. 10.

Nor am I suggesting a subordinate role for the other private, bilateral, and UN agencies—a role these agencies would simply never accept and one that would probably cause their sources of funding to dry up. Rather, UNDRO should serve as a disaster relief traffic policeman, controlling the flow of information, supplies, and equipment. It was conceived originally to perform just this function, but it has never been given the authority or resources necessary to fulfill its mandate.

The following modifications to the current international disaster relief system would help eliminate waste and inefficiency:

1) When a disaster occurs, all information about casualties and damage should be made available to the national disaster relief organization, if one exists. If there is none, the national government should appoint one of its existing agencies as the in-country focal point for relief coordination. While the national Red Cross society, local church organizations, and other concerned private groups and foreign embassies may and certainly will transmit information about damage and relief requirements to their overseas headquarters, this information must be sent simultaneously to the national organization, where it should be correlated into one authoritative (a) damage and casualty assessment and (b) list of relief requirements.

2) The national relief organization should designate one foreign assistance agency to assist in coordinating foreign relief assistance within that country. In most instances, the UNDP—through its Resident Representative (ResRep)—will be best suited to fill this role. The ResRep can tap the resources of a combined UN "country team" of technical agency representatives and can act as an executive assistant for foreign relief coordination to the director of the national organization. The national organization, or the UNDP ResRep acting on its behalf, should be the sole direct information link to UNDRO in Geneva.

3) UNDRO/Geneva should issue an authoritative situation report on the disaster based on the correlated reports of damage and requirements and should distribute it to all concerned multilateral, bilateral, and private organizations. These organizations should contribute to the relief operation in response to needs certified by UNDRO and should inform UNDRO (and the national disaster organization in-country) immediately when a contribution is made. This chain of communication must be maintained, whether a donor is contributing funds

directly or through an affiliated agency in-country—such as a foreign government through its embassy, a national Red Cross society through the local society, a donor church organization through a local church or church council, etc.

4) As a relief operation matures, and as new information about damage accumulates and contributions meet certain relief needs, all reports by agencies monitoring progress should be sent to the national organization or national focal point, for its use and for transmission to UNDRO/Geneva. UNDRO would then issue authoritative revisions of the original situation reports, including lists of contributions received. Donor governments and organizations should also ensure that their own reporting on contributions is consistent with UNDRO's.

Figure 1 depicts my proposal for the flow of information during a major disaster operation requiring international assistance.

Throughout this process, individual donor governments and organizations will undertake independent reporting, fund raising, purchasing, shipping, etc., but both the national organization and UNDRO/Geneva should be aware of every step taken. Further, if a particular government, church, UN agency, etc., plays a major role in a particular disaster operation, arrangements should be made temporarily to lend one of its representatives to both the national organization headquarters in-country and to UNDRO/Geneva.

The proposed system differs only slightly from what is now *theoretically* supposed to happen in the following ways:

1) I am suggesting a rigid and uniform requirement that all relief donor agencies send copies of their reports to the national organization and UNDRO. At present, there is no such requirement. National governments in disaster-prone countries might consider requiring such reporting arrangements as part of the basic agreements under which these donors establish and maintain a presence in-country.

2) The UNDP ResRep, as representative of UNDRO in-country, does not presently coordinate foreign relief assistance—at least not in most disaster-prone developing countries. I am suggesting that the ResRep undertake the role of a traffic cop or clearinghouse on behalf of the national government concerned, when the national government cannot or does not wish to play that role itself. How much the ResRep then becomes enmeshed in administrative decisions (such

as assigning priority to different relief needs) should and will be the decision of the national government.

3) The UNDP ResRep is currently the direct information link between UNDRO in Geneva and the various entities involved in disaster operations, including the national government of the disaster-stricken country. As national disaster organizations are developed and become more effective, a direct link between those organizations and UNDRO would be preferable. Where the national government wishes it, the UNDP ResRep might assume this responsibility on its behalf. In any event, the national organization and the UN country team headed by the UNDP ResRep should form virtually a single administrative unit during a major relief effort.

4) There are currently no Red Cross or other agency staff seconded to UNDRO on a permanent basis. The League of Red Cross Societies, and perhaps the World Council of Churches as well, should have permanent liaison staff working with UNDRO and available to assist in joint disaster relief coordination missions immediately following a disaster. Beyond this, however, UNDRO should be able to get representatives of other agencies temporarily assigned to help in particular relief efforts. For instance, in the case of a drought, UNDRO should be able to receive staff assistance from FAO and WFP; or if a disaster occurs in a Latin American country, it should be able to call upon a concerned private organization such as the Catholic church.

Preparedness Prevention

No amount of reform and reorganization in Geneva and New York is going to improve substantially the speed and efficiency with which relief actually gets to disaster victims unless ways are found to improve uniformly the administrative and logistical capacities of national governments and relief organizations in the disaster-prone countries.

It is the national government disaster relief organization, from the village level to the administrative center in the capital city, that must originate and refine the initial damage reports and assessments of relief needs, produce the trained personnel to manage and implement operations, and take primary responsibility for internal receipt, sorting, transportation, and distribution of relief equipment and supplies. The government then bears major responsibility for the various kinds of monitoring and reporting (to UNDRO) that are essential later in the

FIGURE 1

The Proposed Flow of Information
Following a Major Natural Disaster

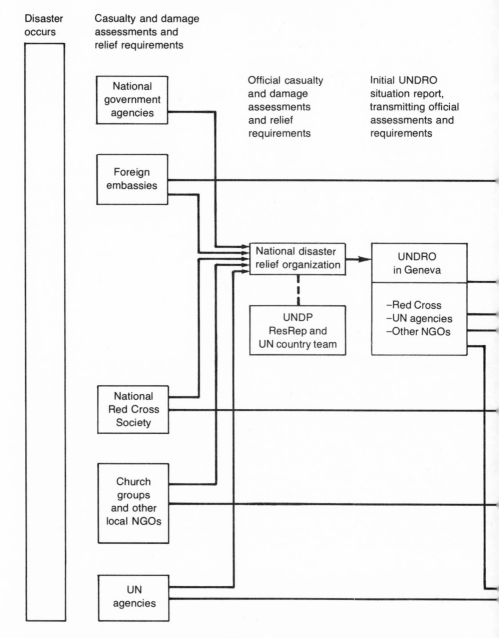

Information on
funds, equipment,
and supplies pur-
chased and shipped

Official
information on
relief received
and distributed

Subsequent UNDRO situation
reports on relief supplies pur-
chased, shipped, received, and
distributed

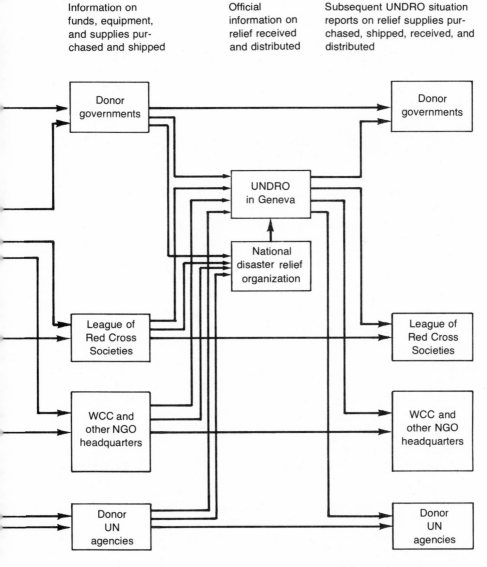

relief operation. No other entity can effectively perform these tasks in a major disaster operation—certainly no foreign agency or combination of agencies. The latter must serve, if they are to serve at all, in auxiliary capacities to the government. If there is any lesson to be derived from recent major international disasters, it is this one.

Preparing to take on such responsibilities is a complex and costly affair for any country—but especially so for the poorest disaster-prone LDCs, whose extreme vulnerability makes preparedness critical. These countries should make preparedness activities an integral part of their national development plan and process.

The same is true of disaster prevention programs. "Prevention" is defined by UNDRO as "the establishment of long-range policies and programs for the application of scientific and technical measures to prevent or eliminate the occurrence of disasters";[24] it includes developing early-warning systems, planning and zoning land use, siting new settlements away from vulnerable areas, reviewing structural design and building specifications, and the like.

Since both preparedness and prevention are expensive and technical, the poorest countries require foreign assistance if they are to undertake such programs systematically. But who is to coordinate preparedness and prevention assistance internationally? Which government or UN agency is to be the focal point for information about existing plans and programs? Who is to determine allocation priorities—in terms of both programs and regions—for the limited assistance funds available? Which agency is to assist national governments in the planning, programming, training, and other field activities?

A variety of governments and organizations obviously must be involved, but the present degree of fractionalization is chaotic and unacceptable. FAO, UNESCO, UNEP, UNDRO, the League, individual donor Red Cross societies, and many other organizations currently scurry in different directions with different concepts of plans and priorities. Often unaware of each other's technical assistance activities, they certainly are not engaged in any global work plan. Donor nations in particular find the lack of such a plan lamentable.[25]

General Assembly Resolution 2816 would appear to settle the matter

---

[24]This quotation is taken from an untitled and undated paper written and circulated by the Chief of UNDRO's Planning and Prevention Division.

[25]*Summary Records, Meeting of 13–14 May 1976, on International Disaster Management*, UNDRO/19/76, GE. 76-5452, undated.

of who should coordinate the UN's disaster preparedness and prevention assistance programs. It designates UNDRO to "promote" these activities, and to "draw upon United Nations resources available for such purposes." But is UNDRO best equipped for this task? Let us examine first the arguments for the primary UNDRO role, then those for transferring UNDRO's function to the United Nations Development Programme (UNDP):

Arguments for UNDRO:

1) The organization that coordinates international assistance to disaster relief operations should also coordinate preparedness and prevention activities. The two roles are complementary: in order most effectively to coordinate relief assistance, UNDRO must also be thoroughly familiar with a country's preparedness and all other disaster-related information.

2) UNDRO's responsibility for preparedness and prevention activities makes these efforts more visible than they would be if buried among UNDP's many development assistance concerns. Thus, it is easier to fund and mount a global program of assistance through UNDRO.

3) UNDRO has already been mandated this responsibility by General Assembly Resolution 2816 but has never been given sufficient resources to fulfill its order. Now, just as UNDRO and these resources are being expanded, is no time to transfer the responsibility to another agency.

Arguments for UNDP:

1) International assistance to national disaster preparedness/prevention activities is essentially a programming and planning exercise. The agency administering that assistance must have close ties to government planning ministries and a permanent in-country presence in order to undertake such actions as assuring that material assistance arrives, monitoring training and other activities, and reporting to donor sources on progress. UNDRO does not have these contacts or permanent presence, nor will it in the future. UNDP has them now.

2) The expertise required for technical assistance to many different prevention programs—early-warning systems, laws regarding architectural design restrictions, flood plain zoning, and other matters—lies with UN agencies such as WMO, ITU, UNESCO, etc. UNDRO cannot orchestrate the activities of these sister agencies. UNDP, as

the central UN development assistance agency, can do so and in fact already does, in the context of other types of development assistance projects.

3) UNDP already is experienced in dealing with major donor sources—governments, world and regional development banks, etc. To enmesh UNDRO in the funding and management of a form of development assistance is to try to reinvent the wheel and to create unnecessary duplication.

4) Only when governments of developing countries make preparedness/prevention activities their priority will the pace accelerate on a global scale. Thus, governments—particularly those that have not recently had major natural disasters—must first be persuaded that it is in their interest to undertake such efforts. UNDP has the contacts *and influence* to do this; UNDRO does not.

Were the UNDP to assume this preparedness/prevention task, there would be need, certainly, for cooperation between the two agencies. UNDRO would continue to play a research and demonstration role for UN field activities while UNDP implemented assistance programs. This might mean amending Resolution 2816 slightly to limit UNDRO's role essentially to research and demonstration and to specify UNDP's responsibilities for implementation of all UN-assisted programs. UNDRO would provide technical assistance for some preparedness programs, develop pilot programs, investigate new approaches, and disseminate information on activities in the field. UNDP would work directly with national planning ministries, obtain funding, and monitor and report to funding sources on the status of individual projects.

The League of Red Cross Societies should also play an important role in this field. Some 122 national governments, including those of virtually all the disaster-prone countries, depend very heavily on their national Red Cross societies to mobilize relief assistance. The particular strength of the Red Cross is its emphasis on people and voluntary activity. In any major disaster, the vast proportion of relief efforts will always be voluntary. No nation can afford to have a paid relief "establishment" in waiting sufficient to handle all or even most of the myriad relief tasks; certainly no Third or Fourth World nation can afford this.

The League's relationship with national Red Cross societies regarding research, development, coordination, and assistance should be similar to that which the UN has with national governments. In fact, the

League and UNDRO should undertake joint efforts, since national disaster plans and organizations must incorporate both governmental and (national) Red Cross capacities.

The proposed international system for assistance to preparedness/prevention activities is represented in Figure 2.

In addition to this general administrative reorganization, special attention should be given to the development of early-warning systems for food production shortfalls and communicable disease epidemics. The UN should convene and the relevant UN technical agencies should sponsor the diplomatic conferences necessary to obtain the cooperation of governments in the automatic information-sharing systems that are the basis for any global early-warning scheme. The related UN technical agencies should be the focal points for the maintenance of such schemes, just as WMO now is for the World Weather Watch, WHO for communicable diseases, FAO for food production, and so on. But governments must be formally committed to the schemes, and UNDP should assist them financially to undertake this commitment.

The nature of the working agreements between the governments and these agencies is important. I would suggest a series of bilateral agreements between technical ministries (or services within ministries) and the UN technical agencies—for instance, between the Epidemiological Division of the Ministry of Public Health of country X and the WHO.

FIGURE 2

**Proposed International System for
Assistance to Preparedness/Prevention Activities**

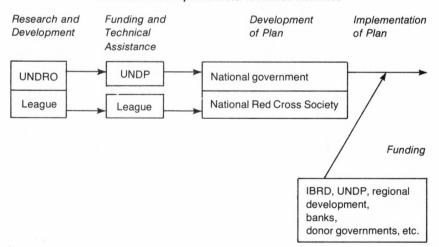

Such agreements would substantially strengthen (in this case) the international communicable disease early-warning system and would help prevent calamities such as the Ethiopian cholera epidemic of 1973.

The aim would be to establish early-warning systems on a technical, not a diplomatic, level so that the reporting involved would be seen as a scientific exercise of common benefit to all nations, rather than a form of violation of national sovereignty. Such an arrangement is not without precedent: in 1962, Cuba and the United States continued to send each other accurate weather data with direct military application throughout the entire missile crisis. The exchange was prearranged as part of WMO's World Weather Watch project.

SIX

The Dark Side of Relief

In an ideal world—one populated entirely by rational, humane people—the predictions and prescriptions in the previous section could conclude this paper. In such a world, the resolution of disaster relief management problems would suffice to produce a working international disaster relief system. When an earthquake occurred, signs of an imminent famine appeared, or a civil war caused massive suffering by civilians, the affected governments would notify UNDRO and a major relief operation would be swiftly and efficiently mounted. Professional assessments of damage, lists of requirements, interagency and intergovernmental communication, funding, purchasing, shipping—all would happen within hours or days.

But governments and their leaders, like all of us, have their dark side. Natural disaster situations frequently tempt regimes to subordinate the needs of disaster victims to their own perceived interests. And when those temptations prove strong, political and moral crises are added to the more obvious human and economic effects of disasters.

ACKNOWLEDGMENT OF DISASTERS

The most serious aspect of this problem was described by Aaron Ifek-wunigwe in a 1975 report to the UNICEF Executive Board:

International relief agencies usually enter a country only at the invitation of the government. This presupposes that the government recognizes and acknowledges that a problem exists. In many instances, delays in bringing relief have occurred because, for varying reasons, a government has not publicly acknowledged the existence of a disaster.[26]

Observers often assume that mass human suffering is substantially less political in natural disasters than it is in conflict situations. In many, many instances, however, it is not. The cholera epidemic in Guinea (1969), the tidal wave and floods in East Pakistan (1970), the early and middle stages of the drought in the Sahel (1968–1972), the Ethiopian famine and cholera epidemic (1973), the famines in India and Haiti (1975), and the Philippine earthquake (1976) are but a few of the disasters in which politically prompted official resistance prevented or delayed relief operations.

The reasons for the reluctance vary from disaster to disaster and from regime to regime, but patterns are discernible. As one Red Cross observer has noted, epidemics and health emergencies seem to pose particular problems.[27] In some cases—such as Guinea in 1969 and Ethiopia in 1973—the government may have believed, with some justification, that its acknowledgment of a problem such as cholera would result in a reduction in agricultural export sales to countries fearful of importing disease along with bananas or coffee.

Quite often—and this was certainly a factor in Ethiopia—the government does not wish to have the international press and relief agencies discover the shocking inadequacy of health services infrastructures outside the capital city. In a famine, the same point may apply to roads and communications infrastructures—particularly if a government has been spending its foreign aid to improve them with very little effect. The possibility of reduced revenues from tourism may also help convince governments to hide or ignore the existence of famine or disease.

Even if these specific problems do not exist, many governments may try to avoid acknowledging a disaster because of their general fear of attention from the international press. Once reporters come to a country

[26]Aaron Ifekwunigwe, *Emergencies*, vol. IV of *Priorities in Child Nutrition*, Harvard University School of Public Health, Cambridge, Mass., presented to the May 1975 UNICEF Executive Board Session.

[27]Holdsworth, *Red Cross*, p. 45.

to cover one story, they often look around for others. Journalists covering the famine in Ethiopia were the ones who first began to write on the extent of latent opposition to Haile Selassie in his own country. Ferdinand Marcos probably feared a similar occurrence when he prohibited outside assistance to the earthquake victims of Mindanao in 1976. The irony, of course, is that the longer a government allows a disaster situation to go unnoticed and untended, the more newsworthy it becomes. Accusations of criminal negligence or genocide make far better copy than do the logistical details of a relief operation.

It is somewhat ironic that fear of internal political opponents may convince regimes to hide a disaster, for it is not the natural causes or the existence of a food shortage per se that feeds political opposition, but rather a government's failure to act. Only after a government's delay has contributed to the adverse human effects of a disaster is there political hell to pay. Jean Mayer has written persuasively that revolution is more likely to take place *after* a famine, when food is again available, "while the memory of the actual or supposed corruption or incompetence shown by the government is still fresh."[28] The secession of Bangladesh in 1971 and the collapse of Mujib Rahman's government, the fall of Niger's Hamani Diori and Ethiopia's Haile Selassie, and the Indian government's constant difficulties in the famine-wracked state of Gujarat all support this argument.

RELIEF REQUIREMENTS

The initial acknowledgment of a disaster is by no means the only phase in which political factors can sabotage a relief operation. Financially hard-pressed governments are often tempted to use the occasion of a disaster and the subsequent relief operations to help fund items already carried in the national budget. Governments may understate the effects of a disaster for reasons of national pride or overstate damage so that relief supplies of medicine, for instance, may be used for the ordinary operation of hospitals and other institutions.[29]

Such was clearly the case in the 1974 Ethiopian famine, during which the government exaggerated requests for food relief in order to defray

[28]Mayer, "Coping with Famine," p. 101.
[29]Holdsworth, *Red Cross,* p. 53.

costs for previously budgeted grain imports. This act may have seriously affected other disaster-stricken countries, notably Pakistan, which at the time was vying for whatever surplus grain was available from the export countries in a period of tight supplies.

This practice is so common that many relief organizations allow for it when they respond to requests for relief assistance. WHO normally approves all purchases of drugs and medical supplies provided by UN agencies in disaster operations, and at a meeting of relief organizations in Geneva in 1975, the WHO Emergency Coordinator stated that his office, as a general rule, halved the requests for emergency drugs originating in disaster-stricken countries.

PARTIALITY IN RELIEF DISTRIBUTION

After relief operations begin, governments may be selective in the distribution of supplies; they may wish to use human need to bring one or another ethnic group or region to heel or to resettle people in different areas. This practice is most visible where open conflict already exists, such as in Biafra (1969) and Burundi (1972) or currently in Eritrea in Ethiopia. But it may also affect natural disaster operations, as it did with the nomadic tribes on the perimeter of the Sahara in the Sahel drought,[30] and with Indians in the highland interiors of Latin American countries.

Often governments act in good faith—according to what they perceive as the best interests of the needy individuals—when they use relief in this way. The governments of Mali and Somalia, among others, have followed through with resettlement schemes that originated in a famine, on the assumption that the extended drought that existed in certain areas of these countries had actually made them uninhabitable by nomads.

But in other instances, quite different motives have prevailed. The Governor of the Arosa District of Wollo Province in Ethiopia, which is inhabited almost entirely by nomads, risked his life in 1973 by publicly accusing the Christian, Amhara (tribal) regime of Haile Selassie of purposely ignoring the needs of the Moslem, non-Amhara tribes of his district. It was an act of courage made possible only by the fact that the Governor had previously saved the Emperor's life in a helicopter accident.

[30]Morris, *Disaster,* p. 53.

CORRUPTION

Blatant inefficiency and corruption are other political problems that can impede the progress of a relief operation. They not only deprive victims of life-giving relief but can also discourage potential sources of contributions, when known in donor countries.

The international reporting on practically every major disaster operation contains accusations of some form of corruption. Sometimes these reports are unfounded; often they are exaggerated. In all instances, such accusations are newsworthy and represent what people in donor countries suspect is happening to their contributions in the confusion of a disaster operation. Both donor and recipient countries, then, have an interest in some means of independent fact-finding that can confirm or allay these suspicions.

The playing of "politics" in disasters is by no means limited to the governments of the affected countries themselves. Donor governments and organizations have their own reasons for allowing political considerations to influence when, where, and if relief will be given, often without regard for the needs of disaster victims. Thus, donor governments and organizations are only too willing to ignore a disaster, to delay operations, or to overlook irregularities in relief distribution. It is not too cynical to say that political considerations are in fact often the prime motivation for governments (particularly) to provide relief at all. USAID recently admitted as much in a United States government report.[31] In any event, the politics of disasters lies beyond the reach of the present international disaster relief system, and no possible managerial reforms of this system would resolve them.

The most difficult problem faced by an international disaster relief system is that however widely accepted its humanitarian goals may be, its means are frequently perceived as threatening the sovereignty of nation-states. An international consensus that as many lives as possible should be saved in any disaster is meaningless without mechanisms to ensure the possibility of relief—even when there are political obstacles. For a relief system without either regular, accurate access to information on damage assessments and relief requirements or guaranteed transport and communications systems would hardly be effective.

Certainly an international disaster relief system will need the cooperation of nation-states if it is to develop such mechanisms, which must

[31]GAO, *Need for an International Disaster Relief Agency,* p. 55.

ensure—quickly and efficiently—that a disaster is acknowledged, the needs it creates are assessed, and relief is equitably distributed. But managerial reforms among the relief organizations alone are not the answer, since they would do little to diffuse the resistance of nation-states to incursions—real or perceived—on their sovereignty. What is required, then, is an international convention to establish the principle of international responsiblity for disasters and to provide for the instrumentalities necessary to effect that responsibility.

A Proposal

Some means of effecting *shared responsibility* among states for coping with major natural disasters should be worked out. I would suggest a phased approach to establish that international responsibility:

1) The various organizations (multilateral, governmental, and private) that make up the international disaster relief system should confirm an agreement mandating to one agency the authority and responsibility to represent the interests of victims of natural disasters, where and when political considerations impede the provisions of essential relief. That organization should then approach governments for permission to undertake fact-finding when there is substantial reason to believe that disasters are being hidden, that corruption exists in the administration of relief, or that any of the political problems discussed in the previous chapter are extant.

   When, as may often be the case, the government concerned refuses to cooperate with such fact-finding, the designated organization should as a last resort make public whatever *is* known about the situation.

2) In addition to this essentially informal arrangement, the international community should begin to examine various approaches to establish formal international responsibility for disaster relief. One such possible measure would be an international convention through which

signatory states would establish the *principle* of international responsibility for relief of the human effects of major natural disasters. The convention would equate the denial or delay of relief to disaster victims with denial of the most basic of human rights—the right to life. It would also state the economic, social, and political interests of all nations in the speedy mitigation of the human effects of a disaster anywhere.

The convention should also designate an *instrumentality,* then charge and empower it to implement the principle of shared responsibility. The convention could choose among several alternatives. It might ensure only international fact-finding, on the assumption that widespread publicity would itself pressure a disaster-stricken government to act. Or the convention could go beyond this and designate a humanitarian body to supervise relief activities that the UN or some other politically neutral institution would perform. Finally, a means should be found to help ensure compliance with the convention. Any government could sign such a convention and then refuse to apply it, for example, by rejecting fact-finding or supervision of relief operations by the designated humanitarian body.

Several possible types of pressure that might be applied in such situations are discussed above. However, most sanctions are unlikely to be adopted, and none of the ones discussed falls evenly on donor and recipient, on rich and poor countries alike. In the final analysis, the only realistic deterrents are moral suasion and international publicity.

THE PRINCIPLE

The fundamental element of the convention would be a statement of principle asserting *the common responsibility of all people and governments to provide protection and relief to the victims of natural disasters.* The convention might also state that the denial or delay of needed protection/relief constitutes a violation of the basic human right to life, as articulated in Article 3 of the Universal Declaration of Human Rights: "Everyone has the right to life, liberty and security of person." Beyond the definition of the rights of individuals in disaster situations, the convention might, perhaps in a preamble, state the interest of all people and governments in the speedy and effective relief of human suffering, noting the adverse impact these events may have beyond the borders of any one country.

The concept of international responsibility for victims of natural disasters was established by the Red Cross following World War I. In 1921, the International Conference of the Red Cross—composed of representatives of national Red Cross societies as well as of the local governments—passed a resolution calling for "the conclusion of a new Convention tending to a wider recognition of the Red Cross, of its peacetime role, and especially of its function in regard to relief for disaster-stricken populations."[32]

The International Conference passed another resolution in 1924 which called for the Geneva Convention "to be completed by a convention to establish the recognition by governments, of the Red Cross relief action in time of peace."[33]

In 1927, the International Relief Union in Geneva—part of the League of Nations—formulated a convention on relief in natural disasters. Twenty-one nations eventually signed the document, but the Union and the convention (just as the League itself) never really fulfilled their purpose. Both were renounced by signatory nations after World War II.

What was suggested in these resolutions (and what I propose here) is very similar to a principle of international law later enunciated in the 1949 Geneva Conventions. Since these conventions have been ratified by 140 nations, their principles have achieved global acceptance. The 1949 conventions ensure legal protection, including material assistance when required, to certain classes of persons involved in national and international conflicts: the wounded, sick, and shipwrecked members of the warring parties' armed forces; prisoners of war; and civilians. In civil wars within a single state, the 1949 conventions apply but are not binding: governments can accept or refuse an offer of protection/ assistance services by a "protecting power" or humanitarian body.[34]

During the last three years, a diplomatic conference has been debating two protocols to the 1949 conventions, one of which could considerably

---

[32]*International Red Cross Handbook,* Geneva, 1971, p. 489.

[33]Ibid., p. 490.

[34]For an excellent explanation of the concept of protection contained in the 1949 Geneva Conventions, see David Forsythe, "Present Role of the Red Cross in Protection," Background Paper No. 1, Joint Committee for the Reappraisal of the Red Cross, Geneva, 1975, chap. III.

strengthen the effective guarantees of international access for the provision of relief in noninternational conflicts. Article 33 of the draft second protocol reads in part:

If the civilian population is inadequately supplied, in particular, with foodstuffs, clothing, medical and hospital stores and means of shelter, the parties to the conflict shall agree to and facilitate, to the fullest possible extent, those relief actions which are exclusively humanitarian and impartial in character and conducted without any adverse distinction. Relief actions fulfilling the above conditions shall not be regarded as interference in the armed conflict.[35]

Governments will still be debating the protocols in 1977, and it remains to be seen whether they will accept the articles on relief. The discussion to date on related articles would not lead one to be optimistic. In any case, the fact that the ICRC has drafted Article 33 for over 100 governments to discuss does indicate a recognition of the delicate political problems involved in aiding victims of natural disasters. Since natural disasters are often perceived as being less political than conflict situations, governments might well accept international mechanisms for ensuring relief in disasters before they would approve the relief protocol to the 1949 conventions.

THE INSTRUMENTALITY

The convention must not merely be a statement of a principle. It should also mandate to some international body the responsibility and authority to implement the principle. The question is, Which body? A number of alternatives can be found among existing institutions with some actual or potential role in human rights monitoring.

Article 34 of the UN Charter empowers the Security Council to investigate

any dispute or any situation which might lead to international friction or give rise to a dispute, in order to determine whether the continuance of the dispute or situation is likely to endanger the maintenance of international peace and security.

[35]*Commentary to the Draft Additional Protocols to the Geneva Conventions of August 12, 1949,* ICRC, Geneva, 1973, p. 165.

The word "situation" in this article could be interpreted to include some natural disasters, as the last few years have seen numerous instances of disasters leading directly to political instability, international friction, and even conflict.

The Security Council is probably the only existing UN body which in principle could carry out fact-finding or supervise protection/assistance services in a country that had not requested them. All other UN bodies, including UNDRO, would be stopped from such activities by Article 2.7 of the UN Charter, which states, "Nothing contained in the present Charter shall authorize the United Nations to intervene in matters which are essentially within the domestic jurisdiction of any state." The lone exception to this provision is the "peace-keeping" activity of the Security Council, where "intervention" is not excluded. Thus, barring revision of the UN Charter, the Security Council is the only UN agency that could guarantee relief in natural disasters.

This alternative is not without its attractions, for the Security Council would be able to bring considerable pressure to bear on offending governments by calling on UN members to effect "complete or partial interruption of economic relations and of rail, sea, air postal, telegraphic radio and other means of communication, and the severance of diplomatic relations."[36]

Yet the problems with this choice are several. Not all natural disasters involve threats to the peace, and even in the case of those that do, a veto in the Security Council could prevent any action. Most important, the Council could probably not be brought into a political disaster situation early enough to save many lives. By the time a major disaster grew large enough to be considered a source of international friction and a threat to international security, relief for disaster victims would have become an academic matter and the measures taken by the Council fruitless. For the political ramifications of natural disasters come only after the dying has occurred and the government concerned has delayed, misallocated, stolen, or committed other crimes meriting international attention.

A second possibility would be the use of *regional human rights institutions* to monitor and/or supervise disaster situations and relief operations. This alternative has much to recommend it, for such organizations unite countries that have common characteristics of language, culture, law, and political and economic systems. And as a committee of

---

[36] Charter of the United Nations, Article 41.

the U.S. Congress recently noted, ''States are more willing to relinquish some sovereignty to an international agency which reflects their own cultural and legal traditions. For this reason, regional protection of human rights has made considerable progress in recent years.''[37]

The difficulty with this approach is that many disaster-prone regions do not have human rights organizations, nor are they likely to develop them in the foreseeable future. Both Europe and Latin America have human rights commissions with considerable experience in monitoring. The League of Arab States has recently established a human rights organization. But globally, regional human rights institutions would provide very poor coverage.

Beyond that, there is the question of whether, in view of the close ties that the neighbor member states would have with a disaster-stricken state, a regional organization would in fact invoke the convention and intervene. Finally, most regional organizations would be neophytes at the business of relief and would have to work decades to build up the staff, procedures, and working relationships that several of the Red Cross agencies, for instance, already have.

The League of Red Cross Societies should certainly be considered as a third possible instrumentality. As the federating organization of some 122 national Red Cross societies, the League has concentrated on upgrading the work of these societies and on coordinating disaster relief in peacetime. It is in the latter field, as I have indicated, that the League has begun to assume an identity and certain functions of its own beyond those which it has as a federating organization.

The League, however, is a federation, and each of its member national societies is auxiliary to a national government. It is, therefore, subject to many of the same paralyses as is the UN. Currently, the League cannot become involved in any disaster situation, political or not, until a national Red Cross society requests its assistance. This, of course, could be changed by amending the statutes of the League.

The real problem with this third possibility, though, is that dealing with the political problems caused by natural disasters requires skill in protection; yet the League has no experience in that discreet and delicate art. The right of disaster victims to relief is a basic human right. The process of guaranteeing that right involves protection functions,

---

[37]*Human Rights in the World Community: A Call for U.S. Leadership, Report of the Subcommittee on International Organizations and Movements of the Committee on Foreign Affairs,* 93rd Cong., 2d Sess., March 27, 1974, p. 46.

such as negotiating with the government concerned, inspecting the disaster area, and monitoring relief functions, among others. These are not relief or assistance functions per se, but rather precede and are often essential to the effective provision of relief assistance.

Traditionally, the division of responsibilities within the Red Cross movement among the League, the ICRC, and the national societies has been determined by the presence or absence of the need for a neutral intermediary. In practice, the litmus test has often been the presence or absence of conflict. The ICRC has assumed primary responsibility for the protection of classes of persons (prisoners of war, the war wounded, noncombatant civilians, etc.) covered by the Geneva Conventions.

When access is assured and/or official resistance to such services is dissolved, then the problem becomes one of relief operations and logistics. In this phase, the national Red Cross society, with the international assistance of the League in Geneva, has often stepped in to assume primary responsibility. Where the ICRC has not so yielded, and has instead become embroiled in heavy relief operations responsibilities (as in the Nigeria/Biafra war), its protection services have tended to suffer.

I propose that through a new Geneva Convention on international disaster relief, the ICRC's role as a "protector"—or neutral intermediary—be extended to cover the political situations that often accompany natural disasters. Under the new convention, the ICRC would be empowered to "offer," and signatory governments obliged to accept, its fact-finding and (possibly) relief supervision services to the government of any country in which the urgent needs of the victims of natural disasters were not being addressed. The convention might in addition address the details of both the neutral status and free passage of relief personnel and the duty-free importation of relief supplies and equipment.

This new convention would be a dramatic departure from the existing trends in international humanitarian law. Jean Pictet, a principal author of the 1949 Geneva Conventions and a recognized authority in the field, distinguishes between two branches of international humanitarian law: the law of war and the legislation of human rights. Within the "law of war" category, Pictet detects two separate subbranches or traditions:

The law of the Hague, or the law of war properly so-called, determines the rights and duties of belligerents in the conduct of operations and limits the choice of the means of doing harm, [and]

The law of Geneva, or humanitarian law properly so-called, tends to safeguard military personnel placed "hors de combat" as well as persons not taking part in hostilities.[38]

The 1949 conventions have made this second, "Geneva" tradition part of international law and have given the Red Cross (specifically the ICRC) a role in ensuring that the conventions' provisions are carried out.

The second branch of international humanitarian law is the body of conventions and covenants guaranteeing the *human rights* of the individual. These deal with such matters as slavery, genocide, the political rights of women, racial discrimination, freedom of association, and discrimination in education, among others. The UN General Assembly and the Economic and Social Council (ECOSOC) have initiated most of these instruments. Various UN agencies—including the UN Human Rights Commission, ILO, and UNESCO—have drafted the documents and participated in the special conferences called for the purpose of completing them.

Pictet would have us draw a firm line between the law of war and its Geneva subbranch, with the Red Cross as the primary promoting institution, and the peacetime field of human rights, in which the UN is preeminent. Since natural disasters are generally, though not necessarily, a peacetime phenomenon, the UN would seem the logical mechanism through which to establish a convention on the human rights of disaster victims.

I would propose, however, that we cross Pictet's line and expand the Geneva tradition of humanitarian law precisely because the ICRC is manifestly better suited as a monitoring and supervising institution to ensure the protection of the rights of disaster victims.

There is a qualitative difference between the human rights guarantees effectively provided by the Geneva Conventions and those provided by the Universal Declaration and related convenants and conventions. In the latter case, while various instruments have doubtless had their value as standards of behavior (many have been written into national constitutions), they have not become operative. Any provisions for enforcement of UN human rights guarantees, such as complaint procedures and fact-finding, are vitiated by Article 2.7 of the Charter, cited above, but also by the very nature of the UN. It is a large, complicated, multinational body with confused internal lines of authority. It is involved in social,

---

[38]Jean Pictet, *The Principles of International Humanitarian Law,* International Committee of the Red Cross, Geneva, 1966, pp. 10–11.

legal, political, and economic affairs, often in a controversial way. The only thing more confused than the UN itself is its image. These problems can make the UN ineffective when human rights matters reach a crisis stage.

The ICRC, on the other hand, is concerned uniquely with humanitarian matters. It is small, neutral, and quite independent. Its proven discretion and usefulness to governments stretch back over 100 years. Unlike the regional human rights institution, the Security Council, or other possible instrumentalities, the ICRC also has considerable experience and expertise in the relief field. And through its association with the League of Red Cross Societies and the national societies themselves, it has resources in the specific field of natural disaster relief.

The ICRC would be empowered to offer the following protection services: (1) certifying that a disaster has occurred when the government of the affected territory will not do so, (2) supervising the initial stages of relief to ensure that operations do in fact get under way, (3) monitoring relief operations to ensure that irregularities do not occur, that the relief is distributed impartially according to need, etc. Where necessary, the ICRC could call on other elements of the Red Cross and on the UN to provide additional technical or logistical assistance.

There will no doubt be some resistance within the Red Cross to the proposal made here. The ICRC itself, for instance, may not welcome the suggestion that its protection functions be extended to cover the political aspects of disasters. The ICRC is already overextended as it tries to fulfill its obligations under existing conventions and pursue its work with political detainees. Moreover, the League may not entirely welcome the suggestion that the ICRC's mandate be extended to include what until now had been considered *relief* matters and thus within its own (and the national Red Cross societies') purview.

Yet this proposal's suggested new role for ICRC is quite consistent with several of the key recommendations made in the Red Cross's own recently completed three-year-long internal reappraisal. That study's final report recommended, among other things, that the Red Cross:

- Should be more assertive in the development of international humanitarian law
- Should take a wider view of the possibilities open to it in the assistance field

- Should seek to establish itself as the leading nongovernmental organization within whatever international disaster relief system evolves in the coming years
- Should be more dynamic in its protection efforts[39]

The final report also specifically recommends the idea of an international relief convention to outline the duties of states in natural disasters as well as conflicts.[40]

But what muscle could the ICRC have? If by "muscle" we mean enforcement powers, then clearly it could have little or none. Even those obligatory provisions of the existing 1949 Geneva Conventions requiring the warring parties to accept the ICRC's services (Third Convention, Part I, Article 10) cannot be enforced if the warring parties are determined to prevent by force the ICRC's entry.[41]

Economic sanctions might be imposed if the ICRC disclosed that the human rights of disaster victims were being violated. In fact, the U.S. Congress passed legislation in 1975 which might easily be broadened to cover disaster stituations.[42] These amendments to the Foreign Assistance Act of 1961 provide for the reduction or elimination of foreign economic assistance to a recipient country that "engages in a consistent pattern of gross violations of human rights." A proposal to extend these provisions to military assistance has been made and is likely to be passed soon. ICRC certification that the rights of disaster victims are being violated could be made the trip mechanism for these provisions. In fact, such an arrangement has already been drafted into another amendment to the current version of the Foreign Assistance Act: "In deciding if any government falls within such provisions, consideration must be given to the extent of its cooperation with [human rights] investigations by international agencies."[43]

[39]Tansley, *Agenda for Red Cross,* chap. 8.

[40]Ibid., p. 80.

[41]Part I, Articles 8-10, is of the Third Convention, the "Geneva Convention Relative to the Treatment of Prisoners of War of August 12, 1949," which is appended as Appendix C. These Articles of the General Provision of the Third Convention define the circumstances under which Protecting Powers or the ICRC may exercise a "right of initiative" and intervene to verify and ensure the conditions and respect for the rights of prisoners of war.

[42]Public Law 94-161, December 20, 1975.

[43]*Conference Report on International Development and Food Assistance Act of 1975,* 94th Cong., 1st Sess., December 4, 1975, p. 32.

Similar provisions could be established by other organizations covering foreign assistance from donor countries. And world and regional development banks might enact similar measures. Donor nations, however, will probably not accept the idea of economic sanctions, and developing nations will almost certainly reject it.

The problem with such sanctions, of course, is that they would not apply evenly to rich and poor countries alike. Further, the very threat of such restrictions on foreign aid would probably tend to polarize governments of the North and South on the issue of the disaster relief convention itself and effectively prevent any progress toward it.

In effect then, the only reliably available compliance device is the moral suasion of the Red Cross movement in general and the ICRC in particular. In the past, when the Geneva Conventions have been violated, the ICRC has generally preferred to deal with governments discreetly. Occasionally, however, it has publicized its findings. For instance, in the August 1970 *International Review of the Red Cross*, the ICRC listed Israel's open and systematic violations of the 1949 conventions in the territories it occupied after 1967. And in 1975, an ICRC press release described the Committee's futile efforts to get permission from the Ethiopian government to inspect the conditions of Eritrean civilians caught in the civil war. Having met repeated refusals, warned the press release, the ICRC was trying to get neighboring Sudan's permission to enter Eritrea directly. A tough statement indeed and one difficult to imagine coming from any UN agency.

Whether the ICRC could be similarly tough when disaster victims' rights (guaranteed by a convention) were violated is a question only that institution can answer. But I am convinced that only the ICRC may be able to circumvent the political stumbling blocks that have brought needless death and suffering to hundreds of thousands of disaster victims.

AN INTERIM APPROACH

Any attempt to arrive at a new Geneva Convention on relief in natural disasters could take years to bear fruit. Therefore, interim plans should be made to deal with the next decade's disasters.

The various agencies that make up the international disaster relief system should have an informal agreement that one among them will deal with intransigent governments. The Ethiopian and Sahelian famines suggest the need for such an arrangement: no one organization clearly had the authority and responsibility to approach the government directly, and, failing government cooperation, to certify unilaterally that a disaster did exist, that nomads were being purposely denied assistance.

This arrangement should be informal and very low-profile. Governments need not be directly involved and should not be alarmed; for the designation of a certifying or fact-finding agency should not endanger the first, fragile steps toward a convention in which governments will have to be directly involved. Thus, the agency chosen should have experience and credibility with governments and preferably a history of usefulness and discretion. Ideally, of course, it should be the ICRC.

I would propose that the League and the ICRC together—under the aegis of the Coordinating Committee—further amend the agreement between them regarding assistance responsibilities in order to provide for a new ICRC role in natural disasters. The two organizations might agree that the ICRC is best qualified to perform certain protection functions required in some natural disaster situations. The new arrangements might be presented for approval at the next international conference of the Red Cross.

The League and the ICRC might use the existing coordinating forums—the Steering Committee, monthly meeting, conferences sponsored by UNDRO, and others—to inform the UN as well as governmental and private groups of the new arrangement and to ask their cooperation in providing the ICRC with information concerning possible violations of the rights of victims of natural disasters.

EIGHT

Conclusion

In past years, the international community has looked upon disasters as an isolated problem, and a group of agencies has tried to solve it without any real forethought. I think we must begin to look at natural disaster and the relief it necessitates as a multidimensional event, with different features prominent at various distinct phases and requiring quite different approaches and institutional responses.

Specifically, from the relief standpoint there are four phases:

1) A predisaster phase requiring *preparation and planning*, largely by disaster-prone countries themselves, with national development planning agencies directing their efforts. To the extent that foreign assistance is necessary, the development planning and assistance agencies should be responsible worldwide.

2) A *political* phase that can so prevent, delay, or distort relief operations as to make them virtually ineffective. This phase—though it does not occur in all disaster situations—involves violations of disaster victims' rights and must be met by monitoring institutions that can protect these rights globally.

3) An *operations* phase during which coordination among the various national and international relief organizations is absolutely necessary. A central coordinator within the disaster-stricken nation is thus required. Globally, another coordinator must orchestrate all phases of international assistance. Such an agency must be independent and

have ties to the international development assistance system but no technical or national biases.

4) A *reconstruction and rehabilitation* phase, during which national development planning agencies resume their overall development activities, often with modifications in response to new situations (if any) created by the disaster. Internationally, the foreign assistance required to facilitate this resumption and adjustment must be directed by the major development planning and assistance agencies.

The regime I have recommended here would make different agencies the focal points of the international disaster relief system at different phases of the natural disaster: UNDP in preparation and planning, ICRC in the political phase if it occurred, UNDRO in operations, and UNDP in reconstruction and rehabilitation.

The future effectiveness of the international disaster relief system depends first upon how quickly and how well we empower and enable these agencies to assume these roles and second upon how smoothly they transfer responsibility from one to another as the disaster passes through its various stages.

*   *   *

Certain human problems are by definition international. A large-scale conflict is such a problem, whether or not it crosses the borders of two or more nations. The massing of refugees is another, as are apartheid or other systems that constitute gross and systematic violations of human rights. A major natural disaster is also such a problem. It almost invariably affects the public health, welfare, economy, food supply, and/or political stability of other countries.

Globally, fluctuating regional and world food supplies, changing climate patterns, and the complex of issues stemming from population growth/energy use/environmental deterioration make our future uncertain. It is naïve to think that we do not face the possibility of megadisasters on an unprecedented scale, at least in terms of their economic and political aftershocks.

The international disaster relief system needed to deal with and mitigate the effects of such disasters neither exists nor is planned. We live, in this sense, in a state of continuous vulnerability.

Appendixes

A. GLOBAL STATISTICS ON DISASTER AND DISASTER RELIEF, 1965–1975

Fiscal Year	Total Number New Disasters	Numbers Killed	Numbers Affected	Assistance from International Community ($ million)	Self-help (In-country) Assistance ($ million)
1965	50	47,000	6,000,000	3.6	—
1966	48	7,000	4,000,000	9.6	—
1967	62	1,422,000	2,000,000	173.2	2,964.7
1968	55	4,000	5,000,000	16.5	607.1
1969	36	1,019,000	32,000,000	95.5	131.0
1970	51	73,000	12,000,000	69.5	96.6
1971	51	522,000	69,000,000	266.6	744.8
1972	30	115,000	37,000,000	582.2	81.0
1973	25	112,000	215,000,000	158.9	658.1
1974	19	101,000	12,000,000	32.3	4.0
1975	27	41,000	45,000,000	197.8	64.6
Total	454	3,633,000	439,000,000	1,605.7	5,351.9

SOURCE: Office of Foreign Disaster Assistance, USAID, Washington, D.C.

B. UN GENERAL ASSEMBLY RESOLUTION 2816—
ASSISTANCE IN CASES OF NATURAL DISASTER
AND OTHER DISASTER SITUATIONS

The General Assembly,

Bearing in mind that through history natural disasters and emergency situations have inflicted heavy loss of life and property, affecting every people and every country,

Aware of and concerned about the suffering caused by natural disasters and the serious economic and social consequences for all, especially the developing countries,

Also aware of the varying needs of nations experiencing such disorders, which present new challenges for international co-operation,

Concerned about the ability of the international community to come to the aid of countries in a disaster situation,

Recalling its resolutions 2034 (XX) of 7 December 1965, 2435 (XXIII) of 19 December 1968, 2608 (XXIV) of 16 December 1969 and 2717 (XXV) of 15 December 1970, and Economic and Social Council resolutions 1533 (XLIX) of 23 July 1970 and 1546 (XLIX) of 30 July 1970 on assistance in cases of natural disaster,

Expressing appreciation of the Secretary-General's comprehensive report[21] and of its perceptive examination of all aspects of the question, and taking note of the relevant passage in his statement to the Economic and Social Council on 5 July 1971,[22]

Taking note of Economic and Social Council resolution 1612 (LI) of 23 July 1971 on assistance in cases of natural disaster and other emergency situations,

Noting the study, annexed to the Secretary-General's report, on the legal status of disaster relief units made available through the United Nations,[23]

Mindful of the need to strengthen and make more effective the

---

[21]E/4994.

[22]See *Official Records of the Economic and Social Council, Fifty-first Session,* 1773rd meeting.

[23]E/4994, annex III.

collective efforts of the international community, and particularly the United Nations system, in the field of international disaster assistance,

Bearing in mind that assistance provided at the request of the stricken countries, without prejudice to their individual country programmes under the United Nations Development Programme, can be an effective contribution to the rehabilitation and development of the stricken areas,

Bearing in mind also that the possible response of the International Bank for Reconstruction and Development and other credit organizations and development agencies to a request from the Governments concerned for complementary assistance to the stricken areas, without prejudice to the assistance provided by those organizations for the normal development programmes of the stricken countries, can be an important element in the reconstruction and development of those areas,

Noting the competence of the United Nations and its related agencies, the United Nations Children's Fund, the United Nations High Commissioner for Refugees and the World Food Programme to render assistance in cases of natural disaster and other disaster situations,

Noting further the key role which the resident representatives of the United Nations Development Programme could play at the country level,

Recognizing the vital role in international relief played by the International Red Cross and other voluntary societies,

Recognizing further the necessity to ensure prompt, effective and efficient response to a Government's need for assistance, at the time of a natural disaster or other disaster situation, that will bring to bear the resources of the United Nations system, prospective donor countries and voluntary agencies,

1) *Calls upon* the Secretary-General to appoint a Disaster Relief Co-ordinator, who will report directly to him and who will be authorized, on his behalf:
   (a) To establish and maintain the closest cooperation with all organizations concerned and to make all feasible advance arrangements with them for the purpose of ensuring the most effective assistance;
   (b) To mobilize, direct and co-ordinate the relief activities of the various organizations of the United Nations system in response to a request for disaster assistance from a stricken State;
   (c) To co-ordinate United Nations assistance with assistance given

by intergovernmental and nongovernmental organizations, in particular by the International Red Cross;

(d) To receive, on behalf of the Secretary-General, contributions offered to him for disaster relief assistance to be carried out by the United Nations, its agencies and programmes for particular emergency situations;

(e) To assist the Government of the stricken country to assess its relief and other needs and to evaluate the priority of those needs, to disseminate that information to prospective donors and others concerned, and to serve as a clearing-house for assistance extended or planned by all sources of external aid;

(f) To promote the study, prevention, control and prediction of natural disasters, including the collection and dissemination of information concerning technological developments;

(g) To assist in providing advice to Governments on pre-disaster planning in association with relevant voluntary organizations, particularly with the League of Red Cross Societies, and to draw upon United Nations resources available for such purposes;

(h) To acquire and disseminate information relevant to planning and co-ordinating disaster relief, including the improvement and establishment of stockpiles in disaster-prone areas, and to prepare suggestions to ensure the most effective use of available resources;

(i) To phase out relief operations under his aegis as the stricken country moves into the stage of rehabilitation and reconstruction, but to continue to interest himself, within the framework of his responsibilities for relief, in the activities of the United Nations agencies concerned with rehabilitation and reconstruction;

(j) To prepare an annual report for the Secretary-General, to be submitted to the Economic and Social Council and to the General Assembly;

2) *Recommends* that the Disaster Relief Coordinator should be appointed by the Secretary-General normally for a term of five years and at a level comparable to that of an Under-Secretary-General of the United Nations;

3) *Endorses* the Secretary-General's proposals for an adequate permanent office in the United Nations which shall be the focal point in the United Nations system for disaster relief matters;

4) *Recommends* that that office should be headed by the Disaster Relief Co-ordinator and located in Geneva, be a distinct element within the United Nations Secretariat and be augmented as necessary by short-term secondment of personnel for individual emergencies;

5) *Requests* the Secretary-General to prepare for the Economic and Social Council at its fifty-third session, taking into account any relevant suggestions and the experience gained by the Disaster Relief Co-ordinator, a report on any further steps which may be required to enable the Disaster Relief Co-ordinator adequately to perform the functions entrusted to him under the present resolution;

6) *Further endorses* the plan for a roster of volunteers, to be drawn from experienced staff members of the United Nations system and interested nongovernmental organizations, who could be made available at very short notice;

7) *Recommends* that the Disaster Relief Coordinator should maintain contact with the Governments of States Members of the United Nations or members of specialized agencies or of the International Atomic Energy Agency concerning available aid in emergency situations, such as food supplies, medicines, personnel, transportation and communications, as well as advice to countries in pre-disaster planning and preparedness;

8) *Invites* potential recipient Governments:
   (a) To establish disaster contingency plans with appropriate assistance from the Disaster Relief Coordinator;
   (b) To appoint a single national disaster relief coordinator to facilitate the receipt of international aid in times of emergency;
   (c) To establish stockpiles of emergency supplies, such as tents, blankets, medicines and non-perishable food-stuffs;
   (d) To make necessary arrangements for the training of administrative and relief personnel;
   (e) To consider appropriate legislative or other measures to facilitate the receipt of aid, including overflight and landing rights and necessary privileges and immunities for relief units;
   (f) To improve national disaster warning sytsems;

9) *Invites* potential donor Governments:
   (a) To respond promptly to any call by the Secretary-General or, on his behalf, by the Disaster Relief Co-ordinator;

(b) To consider and to continue offering on a wider basis emergency assistance in disaster situations;

(c) To inform the Disaster Relief Co-ordinator in advance about the facilities and services they might be in a position to provide immediately, including where possible relief units, logistical support and means of effective communication;

10) *Decides* to authorize the Secretary-General to draw on the Working Capital Fund in the amount of $200,000 for emergency assistance in any one year, with a normal ceiling of $20,000 per country in the case of any one disaster;

11) *Further invites* all organizations of the United Nations system and all other organizations involved to co-operate with the Disaster Relief Co-ordinator.

2018th plenary meeting,
14 December 1971.

C. GENEVA CONVENTION RELATIVE TO THE TREATMENT OF PRISONERS OF WAR, AUGUST 12, 1949

PART I
General Provisions

ARTICLE 8

The present Conver:ion shall be applied with the cooperation and under the scrutiny of the Protecting Powers whose duty it is to safeguard the interests of the Parties to the conflict. For this purpose, the Protecting Powers may appoint, apart from their diplomatic or consular staff, delegates from amongst their own nationals or the nationals of other neutral Powers. The said delegates shall be subject to the approval of the Power with which they are to carry out their duties. *Protecting Powers*

The Parties to the conflict shall facilitate to the greatest extent possible the task of the representatives or delegates of the Protecting Powers.

The representatives or delegates of the Protecting Powers shall not in any case exceed their mission under the present Convention. They shall, in particular, take account of the imperative necessities of security of the State wherein they carry out their duties.

ARTICLE 9

The provisions of the present Convention constitute no obstacle to the humanitarian activities which the International Committee of the Red Cross or any other impartial humanitarian organization may, subject to the consent of the Parties to the conflict concerned, undertake for the protection of prisoners of war and for their relief. *Activities of the International Committee of the Red Cross*

ARTICLE 10

The High Contracting Parties may at any time agree to entrust to an organization which offers all guarantees of impartiality and efficacy the duties incumbent on the Protecting Powers by virtue of the Present Convention. *Substitutes for Protecting Powers*

When prisoners of war do not benefit or cease to benefit, no matter for what reason, by the activities of a Protecting Power or of an organization provided for in the first paragraph above, the Detaining Power shall request a neutral State, or such an organization, to undertake the functions performed under the present Convention by a Protecting Power designated by the Parties to a conflict.

If protection cannot be arranged accordingly, the Detaining Power shall request or shall accept, subject to the provisions of this Article, the offer of the services of a humanitarian organization, such as the International Committee of the Red Cross, to assume the humanitarian functions performed by Protecting Powers under the present Convention.

Any neutral Power or any organization invited by the Power concerned or offering itself for these purposes, shall be required to act with a sense of responsibility towards the Party to the conflict on which persons protected by the present Convention depend, and shall be required to furnish sufficient assurances that it is in a position to undertake the appropriate functions and to discharge them impartially.

No derogation from the preceding provisions shall be made by special agreements between Powers one of which is restricted, even temporarily, in its freedom to negotiate with the other Power or its allies by reason of military events, more particularly where the whole, or a substantial part, of the territory of the said Power is occupied.

Whenever in the present Convention mention is made of a Protecting Power, such mention applies to substitute organizations in the sense of the present Article.

Glossary

CRS—Catholic Relief Services

CSLP—Center for Short-Lived Phenomena

ECOSOC—United Nations Economic and Social Council

EEC—European Economic Community

FAO—Food and Agriculture Organization

GA—United Nations General Assembly

ICRC—International Committee of the Red Cross

ILO—International Labor Organization

ITU—International Telecommunications Union

LDCs—Less Developed Countries

League—League of Red Cross Societies

LWF—Lutheran World Federation

NGO—Non-governmental Organization

OECD—Organization for Economic Cooperation and Development

OXFAM—Oxford Committee for Famine Relief

UNDP—United Nations Development Programme

UNDRO—United Nations Disaster Relief Office

UNESCO—United Nations Educational, Scientific and Cultural Organization

UNHCR—United Nations High Commission for Refugees

UNICEF—United Nations Children's Fund

USAID—United States Agency for International Development

WCC—World Council of Churches

WFP—World Food Programme

WHO—World Health Organization

WMO—World Meteorological Organization

Selected Bibliography

DISASTERS OF THE PAST AND FUTURE

Assistance in Cases of Natural Disaster, Report of the UN Disaster Relief Coordinator, UN General Assembly Documents A/10079 of May 6, 1975, and A/31/88 of May 12, 1976.

Brown, Lester, *By Bread Alone*, Praeger Publishers, Inc., New York, 1974.

Climate Change, Food Production and Interstate Conflict, The Rockefeller Foundation (Working Papers), New York, 1976.

Eckholm, Erik P., *Losing Ground*, W. W. Norton and Co., Inc., New York, 1976.

Paddock, William, and Paul Paddock, *Famine, 1975*, Little, Brown, and Company, Boston, 1967.

A Study of Climatological Research as It Pertains to Intelligence Problems, Office of Research and Development of the U.S. Central Intelligence Agency, August 1974.

Tapinos, Georges, *The World in the 1980s: Demographic Perspectives*, trans. Edward Morse, Council on Foreign Relations, New York, 1976. This is a draft discussion paper that will be revised in 1977.

THE ORGANIZATION OF INTERNATIONAL DISASTER RELIEF

Assistance in Case of Natural Disasters, Comprehensive Report of the Secretary-General to the UN Economic and Social Council, UN Document No. E/4994, May 13, 1971.

Holdsworth, David, *Present Role of the Red Cross in Assistance*, Background Paper No. 3, Joint Committee for the Reappraisal of the Red Cross, Geneva, 1975.

Ifekwunigwe, Aaron, *Emergencies*, vol. IV of *Priorities in Child Nutrition*, Harvard University School of Public Health, Cambridge, Mass., presented to the May 1975 UNICEF Executive Board Session.

Mayer, Jean, "Coping with Famine," *Foreign Affairs*, vol. 53, no. 1, October 1974.

Tansley, Donald D., *Final Report: An Agenda for Red Cross*, Joint Committee for the Reappraisal of the Red Cross, Geneva, 1975, p. 79.

THE POLITICAL PROBLEMS OF RELIEF IN CONFLICTS AND DISASTERS

Bowen, Michael, Gary Freeman, and Kay Miller, *Passing By: The United States and Genocide in Burundi, 1972*, Carnegie Endowment for International Peace, Washington, D.C., 1973.

Davis, Morris, *Civil Wars and the Politics of International Relief,* Praeger Publishers, Inc., New York, 1975.

Hentsch, Thierry, *Face au Blocus*, Institut Universitaire des Hautes Etudes Internationales, Geneva, 1973.

Morris, Roger, *Disaster in the Desert,* Carnegie Endowment for International Peace, Washington, D.C., 1974.

LEGAL MEASURES TO ENSURE HUMANITARIAN RELIEF

Brownlie, Ian, "Humanitarian Intervention," in John Norton Moore (ed.), *Law and Civil War in the Modern World*, The Johns Hopkins Press, Baltimore, 1974.

Commentary to the Draft Additional Protocols to the Geneva Conventions of August 12, 1949, International Committee of the Red Cross, Geneva, 1973.

Forsythe, David, *Present Role of the Red Cross in Protection*, Background Paper No. 1, Joint Commitee for the Reappraisal of the Red Cross, Geneva, 1975.

Lillich, Richard B., "Humanitarian Intervention: A Reply to Ian Brownlie and a Plea for Constructive Alternatives," in John Norton Moore (ed.), *Law and Civil War in the Modern World*, The Johns Hopkins Press, Baltimore, 1974.

————— (ed.), *Humanitarian Intervention and the United Nations,* University Press of Virginia, Charlottesville, Va., 1973.

Moore, John Norton (ed.), *Law and Civil War in the Modern World*, The Johns Hopkins Press, Baltimore, 1974.

Patrnogic, Jovica, *Protection de l'homme pendant les catastrophes naturelles,* paper for the Institut International de Droit Humanitaire, Geneva, May 1975.

Pictet, Jean, *The Principles of International Humanitarian Law*, International Committee of the Red Cross, Geneva, 1973.

Riesman, Michael, "Humanitarian Intervention to Protect the Ibos," in Richard B. Lillich (ed.), *Humanitarian Intervention and the United Nations,* University Press of Virginia, Charlottesville, Va., 1973.

Index

About the Author

Stephen Green is project director of a United Nations Association of the United States of America (UNA-USA) Policy Panel on the problems of international disaster relief. He has previously been a Peace Corps volunteer in Niger and worked with the American Friends of the Middle East as Assistant Director of Programs. More recently, he assisted UNICEF in setting up special relief and rehabilitation projects in Indochina and directed that organization's famine relief efforts in Ethiopia. He has published for the *New York Times* (op-editorial page) and the Carnegie Endowment for International Peace, among others.